Is There a Problem, Officer?

Is There a Problem, Officer?

A Cop's Inside Scoop
on Avoiding Traffic Tickets

Officer Steve Pomper

Foreword by Former Officer Lowen Clausen

The Lyons Press
Guilford, Connecticut

An imprint of The Globe Pequot Press

The Lyons Press is an imprint of The Globe Pequot Press.

10 9 8 7 6 5 4 3 2 1

Printed in the United States of America

Cartoons by Benjamin Cote
Designed by Sheryl P. Kober

Library of Congress Cataloging-in-Publication Data

Pomper, Steve.
     Is there a problem, officer? : a cop's inside scoop on avoiding traffic
tickets / Steve Pomper.
        p. cm.
     Includes bibliographical references and index.
     ISBN: 978-1-59921-037-7
     1. Traffic violations—United States—Popular works. I. Title.
HV6424.P65 2007
364.1'47—dc22
                                                    2006015761

For Jody

Contents

Acknowledgments   xi

Foreword by Lowen Clausen   xiii

Introduction   xv

Chapter 1: How to Survive a Traffic Stop   1
The difference between a ticket and a warning
Miscommunication as an obstacle
Officers are people just like you

Chapter 2: Good Afternoon—Do You Know Why   6
I Stopped You?
Different types of agencies
Public safety as a mission
Education is an officer's primary goal

Chapter 3: Hello, Officer . . . I Don't Mean to Offend You,   16
but You're a Liar
Accusatory words get you nowhere fast
Cops are trained to look for infractions
Police myths debunked

Chapter 4: Don't You Have Anything Better to Do?   25
Accepting responsibility for your own actions
The three levels of traffic enforcement
Laws are created for specific reasons

Chapter 5: My Secret Formula   33
Learning the tricks of the trade
Public safety and imminent danger
"Inadvertent" versus "intentional" infractions

Chapter 6: Excuses Are Like Opinions—and You
Know What Opinions Are Like   42
The art of the perfect excuse
Officers make great observations
Pathetic (but unfortunately real) excuses

Chapter 7: I Was Just on My Way to . . .   57
More outrageous excuses actually used
Bicyclists, pedestrians, and motorists
The real power of bicycle and motorcycle cops

Chapter 8: You Only Stopped Me Because . . .   66
Tickets and race, gender, and ethnic issues
Tickets and licenses and registrations
Staying in your car for safety's sake

Chapter 9: Talk to My Lawyer   75
Lawyers are not intimidating to cops
Big egos equal big tickets
Lawyers tend to give the same advice cops give

Chapter 10: Only Hot Chicks Get Warnings   83
Beauty is in the eye of the beholder
Attitude weighs more heavily than looks do
The attitude test

Chapter 11: I've Been Driving Since Before You Were Born!   90
Acknowledging deteriorating driving skills
Retaking driving tests
We'll all be "Sunday drivers" someday

Chapter 12: Honesty Is the Best Policy   100
How *not* to incriminate yourself
Life will be easier when you admit you're wrong
Cops are experts at detecting lies

Chapter 13: Petty Tyrants   108

Definition of a petty tyrant

Why some cops are petty tyrants

How to keep petty tyrants happy

Chapter 14: Alive Is a Good Thing to Be   114

Officer safety is a top priority

Determining threat levels

Officers are held to impossible standards

Chapter 15: Please Press Hard, Officer—Four Copies   126

Officers write other officers tickets

The importance of discretion

If a cop won't stand up against a bad law, who will?

Chapter 16: You Never Know   132

Things are not always as they appear

Assumptions during traffic violations

Crisis, trauma, stress, back to work

Chapter 17: I Am So a Cop—Really!   142

A matter of respect

An officer is an officer

Pull over when you see blue lights!

Chapter 18: Electra Glide in View   150

Motorcycle cops' primary mission

Motorcycle cop stereotypes

Advantages for them, disadvantages for you

Chapter 19: That Jalopy of Yours   158

Be organized with your vehicle paperwork

Don't give a cop a reason to pull you over

Keep your vehicle in good working order

Chapter 20: Born to Be Wild—or Mild   163
Be predictable when you move
Remove your helmet
Keep your documents handy

Chapter 21: No Good Deed Goes Unpunished   170
Most cops *do* have hearts
Cut an officer some slack
The "pay it forward" (or backwards) effect

Chapter 22: Road Rage—Grrrr!   182
Don't get sucked in by a jerk
Remember what Mom taught you: Count to ten
The consequences of losing control on the road

Chapter 23: A Hot Date—in Court   190
Choices you have
People to contact and costs to pay
What to expect while in court

Chapter 24: Are You Challenging Me?   200
Dealing with multiple perspectives
Accidents versus collisions—there's a difference
It may suck, but maybe you really *did* do it

Chapter 25: A Final Oral Warning . . .   207
Common courtesy may get you further than you think
Acting in ways against our intended goals
Working on better communication all around

Afterword   212

Acknowledgments

Writing a book is rewarding, but it is also a long, hard process. Along the way there are many people who help in big and little ways. Regrettably, sometimes smaller contributions can be forgotten. To those who may have slipped through the cracks of my memory-thank you.

To my wife, Jody, thanks for your support and for being such an animated driver; you provided me with entertaining material for this book. To my kids, Bryan, Heather, and Bobby, thanks for your comments, suggestions, and for putting up with looking at the back of my head as I plucked away at the keyboard so many nights. You are, all of you, my life.

These acknowledgments wouldn't be complete without my sincere thanks to Mark Wong, who put up with me as a partner for four years. Thanks, Mark, for reviewing the chapters and for making comments and suggestions as needed, since, for many of the incidents, you were there.

Thank you Lowen Clausen, first for your novels, which I enjoy immensely, and for being so generous with your time, for the advice you gave me, and for writing a fantastic foreword for this book.

I'd like to thank my fellow officers from Seattle--and around the country--many of whom are members of the Iron Pigs (Law Enforcement/Firefighter) Motorcycle Club, for their end of chapter quotes. I am also indebted to Seattle police officers for being there, watching my back, and providing inspiration for many of the incidents described in this book.

To Ann Rule, my gratitude for your interest in my work and for your kind, encouraging words; thanks to Ed McKenna, for your legal expertise and for your sense of humor; and to Tom Hyman for being a patient teacher.

Thank you so much to my incredible agent Sammie Justesen of Northern Lights Literary Agency, for your amazing work on my behalf.

Of course, I have to express my immense appreciation for the folks at The Lyons Press for their confidence in me as a new author. I reserve a special thank you to my editor, Kaleena Cote. As a first-timer, I truly lucked out working with you. You went above and beyond for me and put up with my rookie questions with grace and humor. You made me feel comfortable with the process and helped me to become a more competent writer.

Lowen Clausen

Seattle police officer Steve Pomper has written a book that is funny and serious and always entertaining about that peculiar interaction between the state and its citizens known as the traffic stop. If you follow Steve's advice in *Is There a Problem, Officer?*, you might just receive that warning you want and surely deserve—instead of a costly traffic ticket. If you get the ticket anyway, this book might help you accept it with a measure of stoicism that you didn't know was in you. In fact, this book could also be called *The Zen of the Traffic Ticket*. More important, Steve's book can help bridge the divide of misunderstanding that too often separates citizens from police officers and police officers from citizens.

Steve gives his readers a seldom-seen glimpse into the world of the street cop. Most books, movies, and television series feature police detectives working twenty-four hours a day, eating and breathing the one case they have to work on, while the uniformed cop is the guy who stands around until the experts show up so that he or she can run errands—good enough, perhaps, for make-believe but absurd nonsense for those who want to know how real cops work.

Before you think that here is another "pat-on-the-back cop book," read Steve's chapter about the ticket he received from a state patrol officer for not wearing a helmet. In fact, he was wearing a helmet, but the judge ruled that he wasn't because the specifications had been worn away from the fabric inside the helmet. Or read his descriptions of near-death experiences while riding with his wife, a firefighter, whose trips to the grocery store sound like a race to a five-alarm blaze. Perhaps, like

I do, you will wonder what will happen to him after she reads the whole book.

Readers may be surprised to learn that Steve and most police officers develop an internal code about when to write traffic citations and when to warn, just as they do about nearly all aspects of their job. Some will consider this a proper use of discretion; others will fear that such discretion can too easily become discrimination. Certainly, from my experience as a police officer and from the tales I've heard since leaving the department many years ago, police administrators are determined to restrict such use of discretion. They might not particularly like reading this book in which Steve lays out his code for the reader. I liked it and am heartened that he and many other police officers like him continue to search for the difficult balance between strict enforcement of the law—no matter how trivial—and simple common sense. I hope this book will reach a wide audience—both among citizens and police officers—and it certainly wouldn't hurt if a police chief here and there read it, too.

Lowen Clausen
Author of *First Avenue* and other books

Introduction

Aw, man . . . Why didn't the guys tell me I had jelly on my face?

. . . You don't want a ticket, eh?

Well, maybe I can help you. After writing an article based on this subject for the motorcycle enthusiasts' *American Iron Magazine*, I realized the motoring public at large needed a book about how to avoid traffic tickets. Or at least not talk yourself into one that you might not have gotten had you known a thing or two about what cops have to deal with daily.

There are others out there who could have written a book similar to this one. Every cop has stories like those I'll relate to you in this book, but this is not about the stories in and of themselves but what they can *teach* us about getting and staying on the good side of the officer who has taken the time to stop you. A book like this was long overdue.

There are certain things that have troubled me since becoming a police officer—even some things not related to the upper echelons of the city and department—questions such as why it is that so many motorists act in ways that are in direct opposition to achieving their intended goals? Presumably a motorist who's stopped by the police for a traffic violation hopes to receive a warning rather than a costly citation. Then why is it that some people, even normally good drivers and law-abiding citizens, will say and do things that virtually ensure the officer will slap paper on them?

It's not that I have some overwhelming affection for your average lawbreaker, but I can take sympathy on the normally law-abiding motorist who finds him- or herself on the bright side of an officer's flashing lights. While this book will be invaluable to the average motorist, my secondary—or perhaps I should say *alternate* primary intent—is to make life easier for my fellow law enforcement officers. If the effect of this book is that some motorists will behave in a way that makes an officer's job a bit easier and hopefully a little safer, and if a motorist, whose pre-*Is There a Problem, Officer?* behavior might otherwise have gotten him a ticket, instead gets a break, I'll feel satisfied to have accomplished something worthwhile.

Civilian friends love to tell me about cops who were rude and hardheaded during a traffic stop. Likewise, my fellow cops gripe about obnoxious drivers—and I've met dozens of these drivers myself. It seems morons exist on either side of the thin blue line. Like Rodney King, I too sometimes wonder, *Why can't we all just get along?* Well, the truth is, we can. And after reading this book, you will hopefully have gained insight into a cop's world, well-equipping you for the road. Let *Is There a Problem, Officer?* ride shotgun with you—or stash it away in your glove compartment—and the next time you find yourself in a driving bind, you'll have an edge.

Aside from reading an assortment of sometimes side-splitting, sometimes dead-serious learn-from-your-mistakes anecdotes from me and a number of other officers, you'll get the inside scoop on a few things you've probably never stopped to think about before.

What cops actually do while they're working:

And no, it's not hanging out at the local doughnut shop from nine to five. Most people don't understand exactly what the police do. Unless you've attended the police academy or have a good friend or family member on the force, it's difficult to gain access to certain information. In reality, there's no way an ordinary citizen can comprehend what a cop has to do every day. Hell, even some officers who trade in their patrol cars to climb the ladder of success may quickly forget about life on the streets. *Is There a Problem, Officer?* will open your eyes and let you see for yourself how difficult and demanding being a cop really is.

Why some cops are given a bad rap and why some of us tend to be skeptical in public situations:

Cops these days are besieged from all sides. Citizens' groups, the media, and sometimes even police and city administrators are eager to pounce on any police officer who makes a mistake. Is it any wonder we close ranks and avoid shoptalk with non-cops? My partner once had a law student ride along with him. She'd been assigned to ride along with a police officer to get a street's-eye view of how officers handle their patrol shifts and apply the law in the field. A ride-along is a program most police departments offer, where citizens may apply to ride with an officer for a portion of a patrol shift.

As they headed out onto the street to begin his tour, the first question she asked was how he conducted profile stops. Profile stops refer to racial profiling: the alleged practice of police officers who stop people exclusively because of their race. Racial profiling was a major issue in Seattle at the late 1990s and early 2000s because the city and department were working with community activist groups to conduct a racial profiling study of the Seattle Police Department.

The student's assumption wasn't lost on the officer; her ride nearly ended right there. Being a police officer is a stressful job— especially when people are constantly looking for ways to point out what you've done wrong. Basically we go to work every day with big red targets painted on our chests. That factor alone is enough to change a person's attitude toward strangers. This book will explain in detail that yes, there are good cops and bad cops out there, but most of us *try* to be good. We just want to do our jobs to the best of our abilities and get home safely at the end of our shifts.

How to get into our heads and know what we're thinking before we knock on your vehicle window:

I wrote this book primarily to help motorists better understand how cops think. As you read, try to remember that cops are in most ways *just like you*. They have homes, families, pets, and a social life. They have hopes and aspirations for the future. Sometimes they're in a good mood; on other days they awaken on the wrong side of the bed, just as you do. You also need to remember that we've seen (and heard) almost everything. Sometimes you throw us for a loop, but usually honesty is the best policy. If we've pulled you over, it's probably because you were doing something wrong. And, more than likely, you probably already know the reason why, too.

Keep in mind that it would be so much easier if, in this book, I could make all-encompassing references to local laws and department policies, but that would be impossible. If all law enforcement agencies in America operated under the same umbrella it would be possible, but thankfully, they don't. There are thousands of agencies across this country with significant and varied policy differences. As long as agencies comply with federal and state constitutional limits and local governmental laws, they are free to enact their own policies. The policies in specific areas reflect the demands and preferences of that particular locality. However, how human beings treat each other has certain common denominators that transcend any specific policy differences.

This book deals with emotion, perception, and behavior—and with common sense. How we act and react to circumstances can affect the outcome of a traffic stop. The information in this book would have been as useful to the horse-and-carriage driver in 1806, and the Ford Model A driver in 1906, as it is to today's 2006 motorist, and as it will be to the hovercraft pilot in 2106.

What to say, do, and expect if all else fails and you're slapped with a ticket anyway:

Okay, so maybe you heeded all the great and helpful advice this text has to offer, but regardless—you wound up being stopped by Officer Ticket-No-Matter-What. *Is There a Problem, Officer?* offers up-to-date guidance on what to expect before you even enter the courtroom: who you can expect to see, how long the process will take, and what to anticipate during the hearing, all to ease your mind (and perhaps, make you remember to ease off the gas pedal the next time you hop into your vehicle!).

It's now time to sit back (seat belt on, of course), relax, and get ready to learn tips you never knew, read stories you never thought were possible, and remember lessons to keep you safe and ticket-free so that you'll never glance up in your mirror and have any rearview regrets.

Disclaimer

Although the vignettes in this book are based on actual incidents, names have been changed to protect the innocent, as well as the guilty.

I'll let you decide who's who.

Is There a Problem, Officer?

CHAPTER 1

How to Survive a Traffic Stop

Bus-ted!

In this chapter . . .

☑ The difference between a ticket and a warning

☑ Miscommunication as an obstacle

☑ Officers are people just like you

The day begins like a thousand others:

You've timed your morning down to the last minute. You shower and prepare yourself to be seen in public and then gulp down a quick breakfast. You pour a second cup of coffee, grab your car keys, and zip out the door only two minutes past your target time.

You start the car and let it warm up. Ten seconds—that'll do. You set the radio station and, as AC/DC belts out "Back in Black," you pull out of the driveway, put the car into drive, and head off to the daily grind. You're on autopilot now, with half your brain on the road and the other half on projects that await you and the chores you need to finish after work. You roll down the freeway exit ramp; ten more minutes and you'll be cruising for a parking spot at work.

Suddenly a blue light flashes in your rearview mirror. You glance at the speedometer and quickly lift your accelerator foot. As your speed drops by ten miles per hour, you convince yourself that's what you were driving all along. The lights keep flashing and you ask yourself in a loud whisper, "What's going on here? He couldn't be pulling *me* over—I didn't do anything wrong."

Whoop! Whoop! A quick chirp of the siren announces you are indeed the target. You pull over to the curb and nervously wait for the officer to approach. A dozen thoughts go through your mind: *Why is this cop picking on me? Doesn't he have anything better to do than stop decent, law-abiding citizens on their way to work? This is all about making a quota. This is gonna screw up my insurance rates. I didn't do anything!*

Now you wonder why it takes the officer so long to get out of his car. You check your rearview and side mirrors, but you're subtle; you don't want him to think you're nervous. Nervousness conveys guilt, right? You can't see inside the patrol car because the early-morning sun is shining on the windshield. You hope the officer's in a good mood.

When the officer finally steps out of his patrol car, he's exactly what you expected: tall, fit, wearing a sharp, well-tailored uniform and those signature reflective sunglasses that hide his eyes. The cop shoves his car door shut and swaggers toward you. You time rolling down your window to coincide with his arrival. You place your hands at ten and two on the steering wheel and manufacture a smile. He returns your smile, which seems like a good sign, but who can tell what's going on behind those dark lenses?

"Is there a problem, Officer?"

Miscommunication is the single biggest obstacle between the police and motorists:

Too many citizens think cops are jerks, and too many cops think citizens are idiots. (Of course, some of us do fall into these categories, but that's a different book.) Most people who maintain this skewed perspective have only dealt with a few individuals from the group they disparage. For example, some unlucky citizens have met the officer who says, "I've never given a warning and I'm not about to start with you." This is Officer Tommy Ticketbook, who diligently culls the herd of commuters for drivers who bend the law by even the slightest degree. He's only one cop, but he can stop an awful lot of folks and leave every officer tarnished in the citizens' minds. Officer T. uses no discretion and has a heart of steel; his attitude is: "The law is the law—you break it, you're getting a ticket. I don't care who you are or what you have to say. *This includes you, Mom.*"

This officer doesn't see hardworking fellow citizens just trying to get to work; he sees statistics, or revenue. He stops people for even the most minor violations, and once the vehicle is stopped, he rarely issues a warning. Whether the motorist is a frequent scofflaw or has never been cited after thirty years of driving, it doesn't matter to Officer Ticketbook. You're just one more, big juicy stat.

ENFORCEMENT	FOLLOW-UP
Citation	Pay or Court
Written Warning	None
Oral Warning	None
Fix-It Ticket	Proof to Agency

I'm sorry, but this book won't help you avoid officers like Tommy T., although it might get you one citation instead of three. And who knows—if you follow my advice, he might decide not to give you a "dangerous tire" citation when his courtesy vehicle inspection finds the tread on one of your tires is 1/128th of an inch shy of legal tread depth.

Here's the good news—most officers are amenable to polite motorists and responsible attitudes:

Officers are people just like you, but with a unique and difficult job. Throughout this book I'll ask you to put yourself in the officer's position—and I'll explain what that position is. This is like the old iceberg metaphor: You only see the tip of what the officer is doing; you'll never know 90 percent of what's really going on.

You see a guy walking down the street, seemingly minding his own business. Suddenly patrol cars descend on him and six cops jump out, wrap him up to go, stuff him into a cruiser, and drive away. You go up to a cop and ask, "Why'd they do that? He wasn't doin' nuthin'."

You don't know that at morning roll call the officers received information on a known felon in the area who is wanted for a brutal rape, and whose description matches this harmless-looking guy. Does that change your thinking? I thought it might. Now, back to that warning.

I'll let you in on a little secret:

You've already received a warning from an officer, deputy, or trooper, probably several of them, and you weren't aware of it at the time. Most officers, especially urban patrol officers, look for (or rather, can't avoid seeing) the more flagrant violations, for which they will make a stop. However, during the course of an eight- to twelve-hour shift, officers witness dozens of minor traffic violations. An officer can't possibly stop them all.

Why? Because a patrol officer's main duty is to remain clear to handle 911 emergency calls. They can't be tied up doing traffic stops all day long. And another thing: Most officers don't feel they have the moral authority to enforce the traffic code to that extreme, because even cops are guilty of minor traffic indiscretions from time to time. Let's face it—we violate some minor law almost every time we get behind the wheel. With so many traffic laws on the books, just try to drive for five minutes without breaking one. Just within the Seattle Municipal Code reference sheet I carry with me (which doesn't contain all the infractions), I counted 334 traffic laws available for you to violate while driving. If violating a law while driving isn't enough for you, I counted one hundred parking infractions. But that's an issue for another day.

Who knows? If you drive or have driven within the past fourteen years or so on the roads of the Great Pacific Northwest, perhaps I've already given you a warning and saved you a heck of a lot more than you paid for this book.

YOUR ORAL WARNING:

"It's actually a lot easier to give a warning and then head off to Starbucks. A lot of people still manage to talk themselves into monstrous tickets that they would not otherwise have gotten."

—Officer D. Bunge, Seattle Police Department, Patrol

CHAPTER 2

Good Afternoon–Do You Know Why I Stopped You?

If at first you don't succeed . . .

In this chapter . . .

☑ Different types of agencies

☑ Public safety as a mission

☑ Education is an officer's primary goal

To one degree or another, every size and type of agency is responsible for enforcing traffic codes and laws within its jurisdiction:

If you've been on the wrong side of this question, then maybe you're thinking this book came along too late for you. Well, don't despair. Plenty of cops are still out there just waiting for you to screw up. You may encounter all kinds of law enforcement agencies, from the lonely town marshal to small-town cops, county deputies, big-city gendarmes, and state troopers.

Basic Terms to Know: Officials Who May Issue Tickets for Infractions

Police Officer:	Law enforcement in cities, towns, and some counties
Town Marshal:	Law enforcement in small towns, villages, and some counties in a few states
County Deputy:	County law enforcement serving under a sheriff
Sheriff:	Top law enforcement official in a county, usually elected
State Trooper:	State law enforcement—State Police, State Patrol, Highway Patrol
Park Ranger:	Federal and state law enforcement in state and national parks
Tribal Police:	Indian reservation law enforcement
Federal Police:	Law enforcement on federal property
Railroad Police:	Law enforcement officers—Burlington Northern, Santa Fe, etc.
Port Police:	Law enforcement for air- and seaports

Marshal Dillon may handle traffic enforcement in his rural hamlet by simply walking over to Jasper Jones, the worst driver in town, and snatching him out of his '56 Pontiac Star Chief by one ear. Then, adjusting his grip, the marshal drags Jasper over to the stop sign he just ran and introduces them, up close and personal. When will Marshal Dillon's nephew ever learn?

At the other end of the spectrum, we see Super-Duper Trooper Cooper, who has all sorts of goodies at his disposal: Vehicle Pacing, Unmarked Cars, Radar, Lidar (Light Detection and Ranging; or Laser Imaging Detection and Ranging; another form of radar), plus AWACS (Airborne Warning and Control System) surveillance, and satellite-tracking capabilities. Okay, maybe it's just a couple of Cessna 182s watching you from above, but you get my point.

Other agencies fall between these two extremes, each with their own policies toward traffic enforcement. Though everyone hates getting stopped by the police for a traffic violation, traffic enforcement is an important part of the overall public safety mission. The possibility that a driver could meet Officer Friendly around the next corner helps keep our highways safe.

Education is the foremost duty of traffic officers:

With good, responsible drivers who've made the kind of error we all make at times, a simple oral warning is usually sufficient. I find such drivers chastise themselves more severely than I do. They're embarrassed because they were driving poorly or made an error in judgment. For this driver, a brief lecture is enough; a citation isn't necessary.

> ☑ **Blue Light Bulletin:** The level or intensity of traffic law enforcement depends on the severity of the violation and on the receptiveness or thickheadedness of the driver when an officer tries to educate him.

Then there's the driver who doesn't seem to get it. This could be a new teenage driver who isn't defiant or disrespectful, but still seems a bit ignorant about the nuances of safe driving. For this driver, a written warning may punctuate the day's driving lesson. I hesitate to give the kid a ticket that may affect his parents' insurance bill; plus, why start him off with a bad driving record that could limit his job choices? And we do want him to get a job, so he can pay the taxes that pay our salaries.

For the driver who makes a habit of stretching the traffic code and refuses to admit he's done anything wrong, a simple lecture doesn't work. This driver is incensed that a police officer could possibly question his driving. This driver exhibits the behaviors I'll discuss in following chapters, and these actions will almost ensure he receives a citation instead of a warning. It's never his fault, or he's always got a darn good reason for what he did. He wasn't speeding; he *did* stop at the stop sign; the light wasn't red—it was yellow; and did you see what that other car just did? Slapping paper on this driver is the only way to correct aberrant behavior that puts his fellow drivers at risk.

It's all about strength in safety statistics:

Many people think an officer's gun is the greatest power at his disposal. The power to kill or injure an individual in order to protect himself or the public is obviously a considerable one. But the greatest power a cop has is the authority to stop you while you're conducting your daily routine and admonish you for errant behavior. In other words, to take away your liberty—interrupt your pursuit of happiness, if only for a few minutes—in order to correct behavior that threatens the safety of others on the road. Most law officers respect and use this authority with the utmost discretion. If I'm going to interrupt your pursuit of happiness, I'd better have a damn good reason for doing so.

Several years ago, a visiting police officer from Holland came along with my partner and me for part of our shift as part of a ride-along program. The Dutch officer was friendly and spoke excellent English (decidedly better than my Dutch). He was vacationing in the United States and wanted to see how we do police work in America. One thing struck me more than anything else during our time together. We think of Western European countries as western democracies, or what we call *free* countries, right? And as such, we tend to assume their laws and policies are similar to our own—but I learned otherwise.

"Did you see that?" I asked my partner, pointing to a swerving van in front of us.

"Yep. What the hell was that?" he replied.

Our Dutch police officer passenger leaned forward from the backseat to get a better view.

I shrugged. "A little creative driving—hey, he pays taxes for the whole road, right? Why not use the whole road, then?"

"You gonna stop him?" my partner asked.

"No; not yet. We'll see if he does anything else. It may have just been one of those things—a little glitch. We'll see if he makes a habit of it."

The Dutch officer had a quizzical look on his face and looked as if he wanted to speak, but didn't. "Did you have a question?" I asked, having read his expression in my rearview mirror.

"I was wondering," he said, shifting in his seat. "Why don't you just stop him?"

"Well, that little swerve isn't really much of a reason to pull him over. We're waiting to see if he does anything else."

His quizzical look grew more intense as he thought about what I'd said. "You mean, you need a reason to stop cars here? In Amsterdam I can stop any car at any time I want."

You may not think of it this way, but I took this as a lesson straight out of U.S. Constitution-101. What makes America so special was summed up in that one short question: "You mean, you need a reason to stop people?"

The Dutch officer saw this as a weakness in our ability to perform the job. I explained to him that the U.S. Constitution and the Bill of Rights protect individual liberty. I could tell he was interested, but not convinced. I then said something that upon retrospect was probably insulting, but I don't think he took it that way at the time. I told him law enforcement in totalitarian countries is easy—not to imply that the Netherlands is in any way totalitarian; I was simply making a point—law enforcement in a free country isn't supposed to be easy. At any rate, I think I avoided an international incident, because the officer kindly gave us some nice pins and insignias from the Dutch police at the end of our tour.

You've already earned the ticket once you've been stopped:

Now let's get back to the traffic stop. Once I have a good reason to stop you for a minor traffic violation, I'm inclined to approach the stop with the intention of giving you a warning. See, you're already ahead of the game. Of course, when I was in the Academy, traffic education was emphasized over enforcement through citation. Whether every officer in the field adheres to this concept is another story, but I've maintained it over the years as my own policy when enforcing traffic laws.

> ☑ **Blue Light Bulletin:** You need to be aware that once an officer stops you, you've already earned the ticket. The officer doesn't have to debate, argue, or haggle with you over anything. He can simply collect the necessary information, return to his car, write the citation, get your John Hancock—and just like that, it's over.

Think before you speak:

That's why your words and actions immediately before and during the stop have a great bearing on your quest for a warning instead of a ticket. When you're alerted by a siren's chirp or those dreaded red-and-blue flashing lights in your rearview mirror, the first thing you can do to put the officer in a good mood is to quickly pull to the side of the road and stop. He may simply be trying to pass you and head for an emergency down the road. If he *is* pulling you over, he'll appreciate it if you don't keep driving until you find a place you think is more appropriate to stop. The officer has already determined the safe place to stop; it's where he first turned on his emergency lights.

Once you've pulled over, if you've been stopped by anyone other than Officer Tommy Ticketbook, you're much more likely to get off with a warning if the stop goes something like this:

"Good afternoon. Do you know why I stopped you?" As the officer asks this question, he discreetly checks the interior of the car and the location of your hands.

"Um, I'm not sure." You smile nervously at the officer. The officer isn't offended by nervousness; in fact, we expect at least a little. Heck, I still get nervous when a trooper gets behind me, especially when I'm on my motorcycle. A little nervousness shows me the driver is aware that the interaction is one of consequence.

"Well, the reason I stopped you is that you failed to signal your turn to Cherry Street back there."

You wince, obviously acknowledging that you did indeed forget to use your turn signal. "Oh, I'm sorry, Officer. You're right; I guess I wasn't thinking. I'm sorry—I should be more careful."

"I understand, ma'am; we all make mistakes. Could I please see your license and proof of insurance?"

"Oh, of course, Officer." You take out your license and hand it out the window. Next, you reach up to the visor and retrieve your proof of insurance card from its holder. (This will have a positive impact on the officer. Don't hand your entire wallet to the officer; always take the license out of the holder—you're not conducting a credit card transaction. Believe me; your organization could pay off.) You hand over the insurance card with a smile.

"All right, ma'am. Do you have any outstanding tickets?"

"No, I don't."

"Okay, then. As long as you don't have any outstanding tickets, I'm not planning on giving you a ticket today. Please wait here and I'll be right back."

"Thank you, Officer."

This scenario is in stark contrast to others you'll be treated to as you read this book. As we all know, what we shouldn't do is usually much more amusing than what we should do.

A clever way to guarantee that you won't get a warning:

There is an interesting phenomenon I compare with scolding a child or disciplining a pet in public: It always looks worse to us when someone else does it. We probably look as appalling, or even worse when we do it ourselves.

Well, the same goes for when we watch others drive. When my wife observes a driver making a boneheaded move on the road, she launches into a barrage of expletives designed to instill dread in the most fearless of souls. She behaves as if she's never made a similar mistake in her life—(hold on a sec; I want to make sure she's not nearby). Okay, we all know that's not true now, don't we? Of course she has. This brings to mind one of the more clever ways a motorist came up with to guarantee she wouldn't get off with a warning . . .

I was riding my Harley home one balmy summer evening when I passed a friend of mine—a motorcycle officer from a town neighboring the one in which I live. He had a car stopped and appeared to be writing the driver a ticket; she appeared to be having herself a good cry about it. When my friend saw (or rather, heard) me, he waved me down. I pulled over and waited for him to wrap up his stop. I knew that he was thinking about making a lateral transfer to my department; I figured that's what he wanted to chat about. He finished, I'm sure wished her a "good day," and rolled over to where I was parked.

"So, busy making nice citizens cry, I see," I said as I accepted his handshake.

"Oh yeah, it's what I do. Hey, you gotta hear this one." He parked his bike and doffed his helmet. "Last week we had a meeting about the speeding in this neighborhood at the block-watch captain's house. You know, about people driving too fast with kids, elderly, blah, blah, blah. Anyway, the neighbors voted for a no-tolerance policy for traffic enforcement in their neighborhood:

anyone the cops clocked at six miles over the twenty-five-mile-per-hour limit would receive a ticket—no warnings, no exceptions."

"I take it by her crying she was a victim of that vote?" I asked.

"Worse; the meeting was held at her house. She's the block-watch captain."

I must confess that we shared a chuckle completely at the poor captain's expense.

"How fast was she going?" I asked.

"Eight over—my radar read thirty-three miles per hour."

"Well, she can't say the meeting didn't get results," I said.

"Yeah, I think I made an impression."

Be careful what you wish for . . .

This type of situation is not an isolated one. When I was assigned to the Community Police Team (CPT), I received a number of complaints involving illegally parked, nuisance vehicles in residential neighborhoods. In the CPT unit, officers are not tied down to 911 calls and have time to deal with neighborhood problems that run the gamut from chronic noise complaints to gangs, drugs, and even a parking crisis from time to time. With the parking crunch in many urban areas, these can get serious, and, on occasion, violent.

I'd assure the complainant that I would deal with the issue. My partner and I would arrive and begin enforcement action, citing and impounding cars depending on the severity of the infraction. I can't tell you the number of times the original complainant would come running out of their house asking why we were ticketing or towing their car. We'd explain the violation and they'd often go off on some tangent about having lived in the neighborhood for seventy-five years. Apparently, the longer you live in a neighborhood, the more rights you have to flout the law. We, however, hadn't received the memo on that policy and continued with our enforcement.

I remember talking to one man and reminding him of our initial phone conversation. I'd told him that the enforcement would be fairly and equally meted out. Truth be told, whenever I told someone that, I secretly hoped that they'd drop the issue right there and, instead, we could amend our schedule and head to Starbucks.

So, if you're normally a good person, but you have emotional issues that compel you to act like an idiot when you get stopped by a cop, then read on. Perhaps you'll glean something useful that will help you get off with a warning.

☑ **Blue Light Bulletin:** By the way, contrary to popular belief, crying doesn't usually work, especially for a guy.

YOUR ORAL WARNING:

"But Officer, don't you guys give warnings?"
"Your warning was written on that speed-limit sign you just passed."
— Officer D. Cannon, Seattle Police Department, Harbor Unit

CHAPTER 3

Hello, Officer . . . I Don't Mean to Offend You, but You're a Liar

Another use for Duct Tape: Saving yourself from receiving a ticket.

In this chapter...

☑ Accusatory words get you nowhere fast

☑ Cops are trained to look for infractions

☑ Police myths debunked

"Oh, no, Officer, I did too stop for that stop sign!" The plump, pasty-skinned woman spoke confidently from beneath a white, broad-brimmed hat and from behind dark sunglasses.

"I'm sorry, ma'am, but you failed to come to a complete stop."

"Oh, no, Officer; I'm sure I stopped," the woman challenged, turning her nose up and looking away.

"Ma'am, I was sitting in my patrol car in a stationary position right over there. I had an unobstructed view of your car. I saw quite clearly that you didn't stop."

"But I'm sure I stopped."

"Sorry, ma'am, you didn't."

"Are you sure, Officer?"

"Yes, ma'am, I am."

The woman sat silent for a moment, carefully considering her situation. She slowly turned her head back up toward me and said, "Well—maybe I didn't *stop*-stop, but I stopped."

It's sure hard to argue with her special form of logic. I chose not to and wrote her a ticket. Following her quasi-concession, she began to argue that she truly thought she'd stopped. I explained I'd be concerned about her if she couldn't determine whether or not her vehicle was stopped or in motion. I still remember this encounter even though it occurred over a decade ago. It wasn't the first incident I'd had where a motorist had challenged me over a stop, but it was the earliest one I still remember in detail where the first words out of a motorist's mouth were essentially, "Hello, Officer—nice day, isn't it? Oh, and by the way, I don't mean to offend you, but you're a liar."

Sometimes you bring tickets upon yourself:

It got me to thinking about how motorists act during traffic stops in ways that work against their getting a warning rather than a ticket. Now, maybe it's just me, but it doesn't seem as if using the first few words out of your mouth to call the officer who stopped you a liar is the best way to encourage him to give you a warning instead of slapping a ream of tickets on your backside.

Most people drive to and from work, to get chores done, take the kids to soccer practice or piano lessons, and if you're lucky, to get to your occasional poker game or to get your nails done (gender neither implied nor presumed). Just think about how many times you yell something similar to this out your window: "Hey, Pinhead! Why don't you pull your head out of your rear end and drive like you have an actual destination in mind!" all the while waving your *digitus imputicus* out the window as if it were a magic finger capable of shooting death beams at the offending motorist, blasting him into some hellish oblivion reserved for the worst human scum.

> ☑ **Blue Light Bulletin:** Whenever you're compelled to act uncivil, there's a good chance that person has just committed a traffic infraction for which your local constabulary could stop the motorist and issue a citation.
> ☑ **Bonus Blue Light Bulletin:** Don't take the bait and stick your own head up your derriere. Remember: As any athlete will tell you, the referee (in this case, the officer) is more likely to see the retaliation than the original infraction that inspired it.

Okay, so Pinhead cuts you off: Violation. Pinhead tailgates you: Violation. Pinhead doesn't grant you the right-of-way: Violation. Pinhead ducks his head down below the dash to the passenger's seat to eat his breakfast burrito—well, you get the idea. Ordinary Americans see these examples and myriad others while driving every day. And you're not even out looking for these bad motorists; they find you—don't they?

Spotting violations is our job; spotting liars comes naturally:

Cops are trained to look for this stuff. They see it every day. Still, some folks will go to great lengths to demonstrate that the police have arbitrarily picked them to fabricate a traffic stop.

"Good afternoon, sir. The reason I stopped you is you failed to stop for the red light at East McGraw Street."

"The light was yellow."

"Yes sir, it was yellow, but then it turned red before you drove through the intersection."

"It was still yellow when I went through."

"Sir, for the record, it's also illegal to accelerate through a yellow light. Regardless, I know you ran the red light, because I was going to stop the motorist ahead of you for failing to stop for the red, but I couldn't because I had to wait for your car to pass. If he ran it, then you definitely did."

The man became angry; his face turned beet red and his breathing was loud and raspy. "Then why don't you go after *him*?"

"Like I said, I was about to when you got in the way. I can't get everybody. Sir, I need to see your driver's license and proof of insurance."

"The light was yellow," he said as he snapped his wallet open, exposing his driver's license.

"Please take your license out for me, sir."

I returned to my car, wrote out the citation, and returned to issue it to the motorist. "I just need to get your signature, Mr. Flanders. By signing this—"

"The light was yellow," he said, pretending to ignore my instructions.

"Yes, sir—by signing this you're not admitting any guilt, you're just promising to comply with the instructions on your copy of the citation. You can choose to pay the fine, you can request a mitigation hearing to explain the circumstances, or you can contest the infraction. Do you have any questions?"

Mr. Flanders snatched the ticket book from my hand and signed the citation with a violent flair, slightly tearing the form. "No questions right now—I'll see you in court."

"Yes sir, that's your right," I replied as Mr. Flanders drove off, seething.

Later, in court, I testified to my version of Mr. Flanders's violation in less than a minute. "Thank you, Officer," the judge said. "Mr. Flanders?"

Mr. Flanders set up an easel in the courtroom upon which he placed a large placard displaying a professionally produced photograph of the intersection in question. Upon the display he'd taped several glossy photographs of the intersection, some engineering blueprints, and other notes. The man explained how there was no way he could have committed the violation, and that the officer had targeted him to fill his quota. He'd droned on for fifteen minutes when he paused to glance at another document he'd spread out before him.

The judge pounced on the lull. "Mr. Flanders, we have to move on. I think I have a good idea about what happened, sir; you explained it quite clearly."

"Could I just show you one more thing, Your Honor?"

"What do you have?" the judge asked.

"I've got a videotape." He held up the tape for the judge. A few snickers escaped from the gallery.

"That won't be necessary, Mr. Flanders. Let's move along. Do you have any questions for the officer?"

"Yes, Your Honor, I do." He turned toward me and began to ask a series of innocuous questions. Again, he tested the judge's patience.

"Mr. Flanders, this isn't getting us anywhere. You have one more question, sir," the judge said.

"But Your Honor, I—" he began to protest.

"But nothing, Mr. Flanders—one more question or we're done right now."

Mr. Flanders sighed loudly. Then he calmed himself and appeared supremely smug, like he was about to present the smoking gun right then and there.

"Officer, can you see the picture of the intersection there?" He pointed to his easel.

"Yes."

"Officer, can you tell me where you were positioned before you stopped me?"

"Your Honor?" I looked to the judge for permission to approach the poster. The judge nodded.

"Right here," I said, pointing to the spot with my finger before returning to my seat.

"If you were sitting where you say you were, then how could you see the intersection through all of the leaves on that tree?"

"I stopped you in early January; there were no leaves on that tree at that time of the year. You obviously took that photograph more recently; it's May now."

"Regardless; how could you see me with that tree in your way?"

"The tree wasn't in my way. I positioned my patrol car so I had an unobstructed view of the intersection. It wouldn't make sense for me to set up to monitor the intersection in a position where my view was blocked," I said. Again, snickers arose in the courtroom.

"Mr. Flanders," the judge said, obviously frustrated.

"Your Honor, one more question—please? This'll be it, Your Honor; it's important."

"Yes; I'm sure it is. Okay, but this better be it, Mr. Flanders. I've been patient."

"Yes, sir. How long does the light at that intersection stay yellow, Officer?"

"I don't know," I answered flatly.

Mr. Flanders smiled as if he'd found the chink in my armor after all. "You don't know how long the light stays yellow?"

"I said no. I figure it stays yellow for as long as the city engineers have calculated it needs to so motorists can safely stop for the red light when driving at the speed limit," I said.

"So, you don't know how long—"

"That's enough, Mr. Flanders. I'm ready to make my ruling," the judge said.

"But—" Mr. Flanders began. The judge signaled silence by casting an open palm toward Mr. Flanders.

"Mr. Flanders, I don't think anyone can say I didn't give you a fair hearing. I appreciate your presenting your case here today in such detail. In fact, your presentation has proved one thing quite clearly to me: You failed to stop for the red light on the day in question and you did it in exceptional fashion. Mr. Flanders, I find sufficient facts to find you guilty of having committed the infraction. Please see the clerk before you leave to pay your fine, or to make arrangements for a payment plan—next case."

Frankly, there's no reason for us to lie:

Consider this: If you, as an average driver, see dozens or hundreds or thousands—or maybe on some days, it seems like a million— infractions while you're driving, can you imagine how many you'd see if your job required you to be out on the road for eight to twelve hours per shift—sometimes longer? What if part of your job involved specifically *looking* for traffic offenders? I sure hope you're coming to the conclusion I'm desperately trying to guide you toward: Cops don't have to lie to write as many tickets as they want.

> ☑ **Blue Light Bulletin:** Police officers don't have to fabricate traffic offenses to stop people; people violate traffic laws all the time without any help from the officer.

And it's not about quotas. To paraphrase Clint Eastwood's cop character, Dirty Harry Callahan in the movie, *Dirty Harry*: "Haven't you heard? We don't have quotas anymore; I can write as many tickets as I want."

Hate to burst your bubble, but quotas are now obsolete:

While we're on the subject of quotas, let's briefly discuss them:

> **Quota:** n 1. A proportional share, as of goods, assigned to a group or to each member of a group; an allotment. 2. A production assignment. 3. (a) A number or percentage, especially of people, constituting or designated as an upper limit: a country with strict annual immigration quotas. (b) A number or percentage, especially of people, constituting a required or targeted minimum: a system of quotas for hiring minority applicants. —Dictionary.com

What they are and who uses them is an elusive issue. I've worked for a large urban police department for over thirteen years, and I've never had a ticket quota imposed on me. Furthermore, through membership in the Iron Pigs Motorcycle Club, I know many law enforcement officers from agencies across the country—and none of them issues traffic tickets based on a quota system.

Here's something that might put your mind at ease: If you think quotas are unpopular with drivers, I'm telling you, they're even more unpopular with cops. Police officers like to use their own discretion; they don't like being ordered to write (or not write) traffic tickets.

For example, the 1999/2000 issue of *Land Line Magazine* (a magazine for professional truckers), included a report on House Bill 394 in the Ohio House of Representatives—a bill to outlaw ticket quotas for law enforcement agencies in Ohio. The author stated: "OOIDA's (Owner-Operator Independent Drivers Association) Joan Kasicki tells *Land Line* there is a lot of support for this bill. 'Representatives from the Cleveland Patrolmen's Association, Fraternal Order of Police, Troopers for a Safer Ohio, Mentor Patrolmen's Association, and some individual officers all spoke in favor of the bill,' said Kasicki."

Quotas are a bad idea for everyone involved. Law enforcement for the purpose of raising revenue is unethical. A driver who receives a ticket at 11:55 P.M. on July 31 could call into question the validity and motivation for the stop. He could question whether the officer needed one more ticket to make his monthly quota, keep supervisors off his back, or even to keep his job.

I occasionally meet drivers who think individual officers get a cut of the money raised from each ticket they write. I wish! Just think of the Christmas bonus I could give myself by upping my ticket count during the holiday season.

YOUR ORAL WARNING:

" 'What did you stop me for?' That statement, made to me when I walk up to the window, implies I had no business stopping you. Maybe try 'What did I do wrong, Officer?' instead. This will get you the same answer from the officer, but it sounds a lot better."

—Officer D. Earnest, San Antonio (Texas) Police Department

CHAPTER 4

Don't You Have Anything Better to Do?

Multi-asking . . .for a citation!

In this chapter . . .

☑ Accepting responsibility for your own actions

☑ The three levels of traffic enforcement

☑ Laws are created for specific reasons

This is such a trite, TV-cop-show comment, and I still marvel at its prevalence with motorists when police officers stop them. I assume it's a warning they're after, and if so, why make a statement to the officer that conflicts with the motorist's intended goal? Why not just say, "Hello, Officer. Fine day, eh? I'd like you to give me a warning, but I'm really kind of clueless, so I'm going to insult you instead. Why don't you just give me a ticket; then I can become incensed at your complete lack of discretion and drive off in a huff, and $101 poorer?"

Well, although there are better things I could be doing, most involving activities that are not work-related, and since I'm at work, aside from drinking my coffee and eating my doughnut, no—I guess I don't have anything better to do, right now. You know what? Even if I had something better to do when I initially stopped you, after hearing those words, you can be sure I don't have anything better to do now than to slap you with a big fat ticket.

Remember, when you're stopped, you've already been observed committing the infraction; it's a done deal:

The officer isn't stopping you to investigate whether you did or didn't commit the infraction. He's stopping you because you've already committed it. The officer will then assess several things as he interacts with you, things like: Does the motorist take responsibility for his or her violation? Is he sorry he committed the infraction? Does she promise to try to drive more carefully in the future?

Own up to your mistakes:

A person who acknowledges he has made an error and demonstrates he understands the implications of what he's done, and is apologetic, has demonstrated to me that the second level of traffic enforcement—education—has been effective, and a warning will probably be appropriate.

"Oh Officer, I'm sorry. I can't believe I did that. I don't usually drive like that," Mrs. Balzani prostrates herself before my authority. Not only am I more inclined to give her a warning, but I'm also thinking about giving her my two tickets to the monster truck show on SundAY! SunDAY! SUNDAY!

See, we think like you, too:

In my humble opinion, as I mentioned earlier, there are far too many traffic laws. Too many laws diminish the legitimate foundational laws, causing the good laws to get lost in an ineffective wasteland, as they are often virtually unenforceable and redundant. For example, there has been considerable talk across the country about cell phones and driving. In fact, several jurisdictions have already banned cell-phone use while driving. Cell-phone bans also allow the government to stop a citizen who is not doing something inherently dangerous. It may be potentially dangerous, but no more so than doing many other activities while driving.

Three Levels of Traffic Enforcement:	
Presence:	Motorists routinely improve their driving habits and abort intentional infractions in mid-violation simply upon seeing a patrol car or police motorcycle.
Education:	This is the stop that includes complimentary lectures and friendly oral or written warnings. For motorists who take responsibility for their actions, have not put any actual person or property in jeopardy, and who appear contrite, this enforcement level is sufficient to enhance public safety.
Citation:	This is traffic enforcement's last basic level, reserved for flagrant violators. These are the motorists who negligently, recklessly, or intentionally put people or property at risk. For most drivers, hitting them in the checkbook enhances the traffic safety lesson like nothing else.

Don't get me wrong—I get as frustrated as anyone when Mildred or Fernando drive like idiots while talking on their cell phones. Seattle does not currently have a ban on driving while talking on a cell phone. So, what is an officer to do when Millie cuts someone off while talking on her cell phone? Well, how about making a stop and slapping Millie with a ticket? In my jurisdiction, an effective traffic code already exists. It's called "Inattention to Driving," or, if dangerous enough, it could rise to negligent or reckless driving, which are both criminal offenses. I'll bet you already have similar laws where you live. Many cities, counties, and states have websites that include their traffic codes. Or you can simply ask the next officer, trooper, or deputy you see—but hopefully not after he's stopped you because you weren't paying attention while talking on your cell phone (although this would be an effective way to find out).

No additional law is necessary, and politicians are setting up police officers to be the whipping post for frustrated motorists when they are pulled over solely for talking on their phones and not partaking in actual dangerous behavior. If you expand this logic, instead of sticking to concise, effective catch-all "Driver Inattention" laws, several separate and distinct laws will have to be enacted, such as: Driving While Applying Your Makeup; Driving While Reading a Map, Newspaper, or Book; and don't forget Driving While Ducking Down Below the Dash to Eat Your Breakfast Burrito.

Traffic enforcement is an important part of law enforcement when done for legitimate public-safety purposes:

Most people are fairly responsible motorists, but there is a significant minority of dangerous motorists who routinely put the rest of us at risk. It's the threat of a patrol officer or a motorcycle cop waiting around the next bend that lurks in their minds, and keeps at least some bad drivers from wreaking more havoc than they already do.

"Ma'am, the reason I stopped you is because—" Officer Montgomery begins.

"I know why you stopped me; you got bored, had nothing better to do, and you need to up your ticket quota for the day," the young mother blurts out, interrupting the officer.

"Well, ma'am, I—" the officer tries again.

"I don't want to hear it. Let's get it over with—write me a ticket for whatever you want. That's what you're going to do anyway, isn't it?" The woman's expression hardens as she turns and stares ahead, unblinking.

"Are you finished?" the officer asks. The woman doesn't respond. A child crunches a paper bag as he giggles in a car seat directly behind the driver.

"Good. The reason I stopped you is because I've been following your car from several cars back. Your boy back here has been tossing french fries, one by one, out his window for the last several blocks. I thought you might want to know about it."

The woman's face begins to soften as she turns around and snatches the bag away from Junior. She remains silent for a moment, then begins to speak. "Um, Officer, I—"

"Ma'am," Montgomery interrupts this time. "I'm not sure what interactions you've had with the police in the past that led you to think the worst when I stopped you, but most of us aren't out here to see how many people's days we can ruin. We're out here trying to make sure you get to where you're going safely. You understand?"

The woman nods her head slowly. She appears embarrassed. The officer can't tell whether she's contrite or if she's upset with the officer because he's just embarrassed her.

"Just keep his window up a little more, okay?" The officer begins to walk back to his patrol car, but stops. "Oh, and by the way," he adds, "I could have given you a ticket for throwing debris from your vehicle; it's a hefty one, too. Have a nice day."

"Oh, Officer?" The woman calls out to him, taking the edge off her voice.

"Yes ma'am?"

"You have a nice day, too," she says with a sincere smile and an understanding expression. The officer smiles back, feeling better about the stop.

Another officer stopped a young woman for throwing a cigarette butt from her car. She immediately told the officer that he'd stopped her because he was bored, since throwing a cigarette butt out the window is a petty infraction. The officer explained to her that throwing a cigarette out of a car window can be dangerous. There is the fire danger, and the danger to little kids on the street who might pick up a butt that landed on a sidewalk and burn themselves. It's also a danger to motorcyclists riding behind the offending driver when the lit butt flies back into his lap. You want to see some stunt riding? Set a motor cop's crotch on fire.

She appeared unconvinced and took a stab at an excuse. "Okay, Officer; I usually never do that, so couldn't you just give me a warning?"

"How often do you smoke?" The officer asked in a nonthreatening manner.

"Too much," the woman said with a smile.

"So, you don't normally toss your butts out the window?"

"Oh no, Officer, never," she said, still trying to milk a warning from him.

"Then what do you do with them?"

"What do you mean, Officer?"

"I noticed that your ashtray is clean; it doesn't even have any ash residue in it. If you don't use your ashtray and you don't throw them out the window, then what *do* you do with them?"

The woman's mouth was open as if she intended to speak,

but found no words. After a couple of aborted attempts at speech, she finally said, "I don't like the stale smell in my car."

"Just sit right here, ma'am. I'll be right back."

We're normal people trying to do our jobs, just like you:

I'm telling you, most cops are merely doing their jobs. They're just trying to get back home to their families safely and maybe help a few people along the way. Asking an officer if he's got anything better to do is not only inappropriate and inaccurate—it's also the epitome of rudeness. I'm not sure what it is about being in our cars that makes some of us do things we wouldn't otherwise do. Have you ever yelled at someone in traffic, flipped them off, or retaliated against a tailgater by slamming on your brakes? Yes? Would you ever do those same things while pushing a cart in a grocery store? Probably not.

"Hey, numbskull! Watch how you're pushing that cart. If you bruise my bananas I'm gonna kick you into next week!" you yell through gritted teeth as you skitter down the aisle, middle finger aloft, pushing your own squeaky cart.

> ☑ **Blue Light Bulletin:** Just remember the next time an officer stops you—particularly if you're interested in getting a warning rather than a ticket—he does have something better to do than dealing with your lousy driving skills . . . like staying available to respond to real emergencies.

But if you do insist on talking the officer into writing you a ticket, go ahead and follow this gentleman's lead:

"Why don't you go and arrest some real criminals?" the biker says to the officer.

"Real criminals, eh? Like who?"

"You know, drug dealers, murderers, rapists—"

"Okay sir, you want to make a deal with me?"

"Like what?"

"If you point out a real criminal right now, I won't give you a ticket. I'll just give you a warning and then I'll go and arrest the real criminal."

The motorist sits silently scanning the horizon, straining his eyes for a bit of mayhem; he finds nothing but relative bliss.

"You know, that's the problem with the world today," the officer says, clicking his pen. "There's never a real criminal around when you need one."

YOUR ORAL WARNING:

"If you're a woman, don't cry. I will always write you a ticket. If you have used this before and gotten a warning, not today. Press hard . . . you are making five copies, and the last one is yours."

—Robert Magni, U.S. Customs agent, Florida
(former Oklahoma police officer)

CHAPTER 5

My Secret Formula

"Two outta three means 'yes' to a ticket, okay?"

In this chapter...

- ☑ Learning the tricks of the trade
- ☑ Public safety and imminent danger
- ☑ "Inadvertent" versus "intentional" infractions

> ☑ **Blue Light Bulletin:** Whether consciously or otherwise, every good police officer creates a formula he uses to help him determine who gets a ticket and who gets a warning.

For some cops it's as simple as *If I gotta cough it up, you gotta cough it up.* Registration tabs and proof-of-insurance violations are good examples. Many officers feel warnings for expired tabs and no proof of insurance should not be given because the officers feel the pinch themselves when they renew their own tabs and pay their own premiums, so they expect everyone to pay. I agree to a point. However, every once in a while the universe throws me a curveball just to keep me on my toes. And I know not everyone is in the same boat at the same time.

Giving a warning to someone whose registration expired a few days ago (or even a week ago) seems reasonable to me. Same goes for proof of insurance. If Mr. Tappet shows me an insurance card that expired last month and I can see he's kept every card with the same policy number, for the same car, from the same company for the past three years in his glove compartment, it's more likely than not, he just hasn't put the new card in his car yet. If he has a good driving record and a decent attitude, I have no problem giving him the benefit of the doubt and sending him off with a warning. However, if I stop the same motorist (Mr. Tappet) a second time for the same violation, it's ticket time in Tappetville.

For me, the formula is not a hard-and-fast rule—it's more of a guideline to help keep me consistent:

It has to remain fluid because, as I mentioned above, the universe tends to throw cops wild curves and wicked sliders when we least expect them. Usually it happens just when we begin to think we've seen and heard it all.

My secret formula (okay, I'll come clean: my formula isn't really a secret at all, but I thought it made a cool title) is multi-layered, but relatively simple:

> **Rule #1:** I take into account the imminent danger to people or property the violator's actions have caused. Circumstances or intentions aside, some traffic errors are so inherently dangerous that even when unintentional, public safety dictates the motorist must receive a ticket.

I once stopped a nice woman who was making a right turn on a green light. She failed to yield to a pedestrian walking within a marked crosswalk and nearly struck the lady. I'll bet the middle-aged, slightly plump, and until that moment, slow-moving pedestrian hadn't performed a ballet movement like that in years, launching herself into a modified pirouette as she leapt to safety.

The pleasant and apologetic motorist told me she couldn't see the pedestrian because her car's passenger-side roof strut had blocked her view. Sorry. Not good enough. When you nearly cause a collision with another vehicle or nearly squish some poor, plump pedestrian, chances are you're gonna get a ticket; at least you will from me.

It's all about balancing the good with the bad:

Her infraction was unintentional, but the imminent danger outweighed that fact. And the pedestrian, the careless motorist's victim, expects and deserves to have the law enforced in such an instance.

> **Imminent Danger:** Near injury or damage to an actual person or real property at the scene, at the time.

It can be argued that any time a person runs a stop sign, a red light, or exceeds the speed limit, it constitutes a danger. However, with no person or property actually threatened, that danger is better described as potential, not imminent. You know the admonishment: *You could have hurt someone.* Yeah, but you didn't.

In circumstances absent a real hazard or imminent danger, I use other criteria, such as:

Eddie roars toward the intersection in his V8-powered, bronze 1979 Chevy Camaro. He sees the light turn yellow. The correct and safe thing for Eddie to do is to slow down and to stop for the impending red light. But Eddie has never been a big fan of either the correct or the safe thing to do. He's far too important to have to stop for yet another pesky red light. Nope. Eddie's got a nice cold beer and half a sandwich calling to him from home.

Eddie stomps on the gas, and his classic muscle car screams toward the amber light. The light turns red just before the Camaro blasts through the intersection. Eddie's home-free now; he can already taste his dinner.

"Hello, sir," Officer Horace Portly greets Fast Eddie. "And no, I don't have anything better to do, just in case you were wondering," Officer Portly says preemptively; he's seen Eddie's type before. "I stopped you because you failed to stop for that red light back there."

"It was yellow," Eddie says with conviction.

"Excuse me?"

"The light—it was yellow."

"Well, sir, that's true—it was yellow—then it turned to red and then you promptly drove right on past it."

"No; it was yellow when I passed through it," Eddie says.

"Look, sir, I'm the wrong person to argue with. You must be thinking I'm a judge. You see a gavel on me anywhere? No? I didn't think so. See, if you want to argue so badly, I can't even warn you, because you don't think you did anything wrong. How can I warn you for something you didn't think you did in the first place? Doesn't make much sense now, does it, sir? I'll have to give you a ticket now for sure, to make certain you get your chance to argue—with the judge, not me. For me, I already know you ran the light; no argument is necessary. You get my point—sir?" Portly said as he raised an eyebrow.

"I thought I could make it," Fast Eddie says as he leans forward and taps his head against his steering wheel.

"I bet you did at that."

Eddie hadn't thought about it this way, but he had used the first words out of his mouth to call Officer Portly a liar. Although the infraction was potentially dangerous, there wasn't another vehicle or soul present, in, near, or approaching the intersection at the time of the violation. This is where Rule #2 comes into play: *Was the infraction inadvertent or intentional?*

In Eddie's case, the violation was clearly intentional. It's just another case of beer-and-snack-food-motivated lawlessness. What's Officer Portly's verdict? Eddie—poor schmuck—gets a ticket.

We're not being sneaky; we're simply making you more aware:

Once in a while, I'll position my patrol car at a particular intersection known for its stop-sign violators. Trust me: I'm not there to set up a duck blind so I can see how many tickets I can write.

> ☑ **Blue Light Bulletin:** I'm there to position my car in such a way so that the motorist gets the point as to why I'm there, and adjusts his driving accordingly. I often do this when I have a report to write.

I place my car at the northeast corner where there is a DO NOT ENTER sign preventing northbound traffic. My fully marked patrol car, adorned with its red-and-blue lights sitting atop it like a crown, is in full view of all approaching motorists.

It's fun to watch motorists as they become aware of my presence. They go from speed demon right back to teacher's pet in their high school Driver's Ed class. The car is zipping toward the intersection, the motorist sees me—and suddenly, he slows and comes to a complete stop. (And I do mean a complete stop—a NASCAR pit crew could fuel up and change all the vehicle's tires, and possibly change the oil too, before they drive away from the stop sign.)

Once, after I'd been monitoring this intersection for a while, I'd completed my report and decided I'd leave after the next vehicle passed through. A blue Subaru approached the intersection from the east. It was moving at a good clip. I was looking forward to seeing the look on the driver's face when he saw my patrol car. However, not only did he not see my car and stop, or even slow down, he actually accelerated before he got to the stop sign and blasted on down the road.

"Hello, sir. I stopped you because you failed to stop for the stop sign at Twelfth Avenue."

"Oh no; I stopped."

"Sir, not only did you not stop, you didn't even slow down—you actually sped up as you got to the sign."

"Well, I thought I stopped."

"No sir, I'm afraid not—not even close."

"Officer, where the hell were you hiding, anyway? That was pretty damn sneaky," he said with an utterly baffled expression on his face.

I resisted the urge to laugh, settled for a slight grin, and said, "Tell you what you do the next time you come through that intersection, after stopping at the stop sign, of course, look to your right. You'll see a big, wide-open area with bright white diagonal stripes painted on the pavement, where, if you'd taken the time to look today, you'd have seen me quite easily. Believe me; you're going to feel more than a bit silly. Now, sign here and please press hard, sir—four copies."

Those who fail to learn from history are condemned to repeat it:

Another factor that may affect the outcome of a traffic stop is a motorist's driving history. Different agencies will have different policies and capabilities regarding the ability to retrieve this information in the field. Some agencies have computers in patrol cars, which, when the computers are up, are able to retrieve a motorist's driving record in seconds. Here, in Washington State, law enforcement officers are able to access five years' worth of a motorist's driving record.

If I've stopped a motorist for a minor violation and their driving abstract from the state indicates no accidents, violations, or convictions for the past five years, I'm much more likely to give this motorist the benefit of the doubt and issue a warning, if a warning is an appropriate option for the circumstances. On the other hand, if I've stopped a driver for speeding, let's say eleven miles per hour over the limit on a main arterial, and his abstract shows five speeding tickets over the past five years—one only three months ago—then I'm inclined to issue this motorist a ticket.

His driving history shows that he doesn't take traffic enforcement seriously (or likely, traffic safety), and continues to drive in an unsafe manner. I know that if he continues driving his car or riding his motorcycle like this, he will eventually have his driving privileges suspended or revoked. *Hopefully, before he kills someone.*

Some folks, especially those with bad driving records, may wonder how much information an officer has access to when he stops you for a traffic violation. This really depends on the jurisdiction. Every agency's data retrieval system is dependent on their own department's policies, as well as state and local laws. Some access is also restricted by budgetary constraints; computers and participation in national and regional databases cost money.

Some agencies can access your recent driving record in their patrol cars by computer (although the time frame differs from agency to agency); others depend on dispatchers to radio the information to the officer. Information may include traffic citation convictions and number of accidents. Some agencies may also include information about those stopped but only issued written warnings; however, I'm not aware of any that keep this kind of information. Similarly, I'm not aware of any agencies that track oral warnings in any kind of "official" retrievable database.

Nevertheless, you should be advised that officers do have long memories and a talent for remembering faces. If the officer has stopped you in the past, he's likely to remember you if he stops you again—especially if it's for the same violation. If he gave you a warning the first time, you're probably going to get a ticket this time. It can be argued that it shows a lack of respect for the officer if he's given you a break and some time later, you pass the same area and commit the same infraction.

In some jurisdictions officers have the option of issuing what are commonly referred to as *fix-it tickets*. These are basically warnings as long as the motorist complies with the instructions given. For instance, in some jurisdictions, if you're stopped and found to not have your driver's license, registration, or insurance information in your possession, you may be given twenty-four hours to show up at the police station with the documents. If you comply, the enforcement remains a warning; if you fail to comply, the enforcement becomes a citation.

When I was seventeen I had the ugliest sun-faded, hunter-orange Kawasaki 175 dirt bike. It doesn't hold a candle to my current ride, a 2005 Harley-Davidson FLSTC, but she was my first, and I remember her fondly. I hadn't noticed, but while it was parked in the high school lot, someone had cracked my brake-light lens. I was riding home on a main street when I was stopped by a Massachusetts Registry of Motor Vehicles police officer. He issued me a seven-day fix-it ticket. I was required to get the lens repaired and mail proof (the receipt for the part or repair) to the Registry of Motor Vehicles, which I did.

YOUR ORAL WARNING:

"I stopped a guy for speeding and asked him for his pilot's license. He asked why and I told him because he was flying. He produced a pilot's license; we both laughed, and he drove away ticket-free."

—Sergeant Bud Madgey, Voorhees Twp. Police Department (New Jersey)

CHAPTER 6

Excuses Are Like Opinions—and You Know What Opinions Are Like

"Hey Joe, this one's gonna be good!"

In this chapter . . .

☑ The art of the perfect excuse

☑ Officers make great observations

☑ Pathetic (but unfortunately real) excuses

Officers may respond to several emergencies on a given day, but even on those high-energy days, sometimes the most memorable moment will come during a traffic stop:

The reason: Excuses. (*Sniff!* Do you smell something?)

It's hard to imagine from what realm some excuses—a lot of people have the nerve to call them *reasons*—arrive in our universe. When an officer makes a stop, particularly one that involves motorist impatience, his chances of being mentally sound by career's end decrease each time he's assaulted by what some violators deem an excuse. Some excuses can make an officer's head spin around 360 degrees.

If an excuse is unavoidable:

Believe it or not, most times the best "excuse" is simply the truth. It's amazing what motorists will come up with to try to influence the officer. Officers are very good at detecting a lie. For example, I can't tell you that excuses like "I'm late for work" or "I have an emergency at home" will work better than "I'm late for day care" or "I'm late for a doctor's appointment." There is no set formula on what will work on an officer, because if that's what you're doing, *working* the officer in order to get out of a ticket you've earned, he or she is probably going to know it. Unless you're a very good actor or liar, then, in the case of the latter, you probably have more problems in life than a little traffic ticket.

If you have a reason (excuse . . . whatever), just toss your chips and let them fall as they may. Often it's not the specifics of the excuse you use, but the sincerity with which you present it. I know what you're thinking: *Sincerity—yeah, I can fake that.* With most cops, you probably can't.

An officer stops you for speeding. You weren't tearing up the asphalt, but you were pushing it a bit, so he's initially amenable to the idea of issuing you a warning. He comes up to your window and he finds you—like an old friend of mine used to describe— slapping your knees and squeezing your, *ahem,* because you have to pee so badly.

"Yes, is there a problem, Officer?" you ask as you squirm in your seat, too embarrassed to give the officer the specific reason for your excessive speed.

"You in a hurry for any legitimate reason, sir?"

"Well, um—what the hell, I may as well tell you—I've got to pee like a racehorse." You squeeze your knees together, take a deep breath, but you avoid using your hand to squeeze anything.

"You live close by?"

"Not really; 'bout three miles from here. I was hoping to find a store or restaurant or something." You suck in a deep breath, your decorum now secondary to your most pressing need.

"Look, I'm going to take sympathy on you. I'm going to give you a warning today so you can go and take care of business. Just so you know, I'm not giving you a warning because you have to go, so don't make a habit of using this excuse; I was planning to give you a warning anyway."

"Oh thank you, Officer. Can I go—please?"

"Oh, right. Take a right a block down; there'll be a park on your right with bathrooms."

"Oh man. Thank you sir, thank you!" you say as you drive down the street and disappear around the corner at the next right turn—relief the only thing on your mind.

Like in the story, I wouldn't give someone a warning for this excuse exclusively, but even if I were to write a citation, I might speed up the process a bit out of sympathy or empathy for a common human condition. I understand the cause could be too much coffee or other beverage, but it could also be a medical condition. There's also a certain near-panic sincerity in people who really have to go. As if something inside of us recognizes a true emergency in another person, most people, even police officers, can empathize with this condition; we've all been there at one time or another. It doesn't excuse bad driving, but it might provide a darn good mitigating circumstance—just so long as it's true.

I'd also warn you to really think about what you're telling the officer when you provide him with your excuse (or whatever you want to call it) when you're stopped for a violation. You may also be inadvertently providing him with information he can use to write you additional tickets.

"Sir, the reason I stopped you is you failed to come to a stop at that stop sign back there," the officer says.

"I'm sorry, Officer. I've been having problems with my brakes," the motorist says.

What in the world would you say that for? If it's true, then what the hell are you doing taking a chance driving the thing? If it's only an excuse, then how dim can you be? You've just told the officer that you are driving your car, knowing it's unsafe. In my state, the infraction is called "Moving an unsafe vehicle." I'll bet your state has a similar infraction in its traffic code. Again, you can probably access your traffic code online; if not, go to your public library, or ask the next Officer Friendly you come across.

A few years back I was involved in one of the strangest collision investigations I'd ever seen. I have to admit right off that the driver impressed me to no end for her incredible, almost miraculous feat, right up to and beyond the point when I wrote her a ticket for moving an unsafe vehicle.

I was dispatched to a reported one-vehicle collision, which had rolled over in the roadway with the driver possibly trapped. Let me set the scene for you, as the geography of the location played the primary role in what occurred. Belmont Avenue East runs roughly northwest-bound, down a very steep decline to a T intersection at Lakeview Boulevard East in Seattle. Immediately beyond the "T" of the intersection is a steep drop to six lanes of northbound Interstate 5.

The driver, in her late fifties, had been headed down the hill when she realized that she had almost no brakes. Sharp as a tack, with almost no time to make a decision, she noticed a rock retaining wall which grew level, like a shelf, from the sloped sidewalk in front of an apartment building on the right side of the street. The woman drove her car up the curb, across the planting strip and sidewalk, and carefully guided her brakeless vehicle's right wheels onto the retaining wall and flipped her car over onto its left side. The car slid to a stop between the rockery and a wooden power pole as thick as the trunk of a fifty-foot-tall Douglas-fir.

When I arrived I found the driver, uninjured, standing beside her car. After telling me what had happened, I couldn't help but stare at the flimsy chain-link fence no more than fifteen yards from us and imagine what could have happened had she careened through the intersection and down onto the traffic on I-5. I stood shaking my head as I turned to look at the woman. Her expression told me that she knew what I was thinking.

"Boy, was I lucky," she said.

"Looks like lots of people were lucky," I said, looking past the intersection, beyond the fence to the airspace over the I-5 freeway.

I asked her what happened. She told me that she had just come from picking up her car from the repair shop—for brake work. I asked her if she'd noticed anything wrong with the brakes when she left the shop. She told me that she'd noticed immediately that the brakes weren't working properly. I asked her why she didn't take it right back. She said that she probably should have, but she had things to do.

"I imagine flipping your car over on a sidewalk probably wasn't one of those things, was it?" I asked.

"Not exactly," she admitted with a weak smile, obviously embarrassed.

I asked where she'd taken her car for repairs. She described a repair shop located some six or seven miles south of our location.

We stood silent for a moment, and then I asked her if she'd intended to flip her car or if she'd just lost control and had truly gotten lucky. She said she had intended to hit the wall to stop the car, but did think that it might flip the car; she said it was the only thing she could think of at the time.

I told her that I was impressed, but I was also incensed that she'd knowingly risk driving a car down a hill like that with bad brakes. She could have easily killed herself and potentially many others if she'd done a *Chitty Chitty Bang Bang* out onto I-5. I asked her why, with her brakes so bad, having driven six to seven miles on a relatively level street, she'd take such a chance driving down such a steep hill? She said, "I guess I wasn't thinking." I told her that I was going to have to issue her a citation for moving an unsafe vehicle—I could have written her one for reckless driving, a traffic crime.

I told her that I was impressed with what she'd done to avoid a catastrophe and felt bad that I had to write her a ticket. She told me that she understood, and considering what could have happened, she was getting off easy.

There are obviously too many excuses to list and take on individually here, but there are some that crop up more often than others. See if these look familiar:

- I'm late for work.
- I have an important meeting.
- I have sick kids/elderly parents at home.
- I'm late for day care.
- There's an emergency at home.
- I was only going as fast as the car in front of me.
- The car behind me was tailgating.
- I just got off the freeway/highway/expressway/turnpike.
- I don't know where my mind was.
- I'm just tired.

Are any of these excuses really worth it?

Some of these excuses will undoubtedly sound familiar to many of you. Again, as with the woman with the bad brakes, when you tell the officer the reason you committed the infraction was because you were too tired, too distracted, or your brakes have been a bit funky, what you're really saying is that you were intentionally being an unsafe driver.

Many people using this type of excuse aren't telling the truth anyway. They'd just rather divert the blame from their having committed the infraction while possessed of their full faculties to having done so when they weren't at their best. As if the officer will excuse the action more in such instances. How about trying the truth and a little contrition?

Motorists will come up with some excuses designed to elicit an officer's sympathy:

- But Officer, my husband/wife/dad/mom/cockatoo will kill me if I'm late.
- Do you know what this'll do to my insurance rates?
- If I get another ticket, I'll lose my license.
- If I get another ticket, I'll lose my job.
- I couldn't afford to get my tabs/insurance renewed.

What do I say to these folks? "Perhaps you should have thought about that *before* you committed the infraction." Now, I'm primarily talking about motorists who commit the more-blatant violations, such as flagrant running of stop signs and red lights, speeding, and long-since-expired registration tabs.

They are either driving like dangerous idiots, or are scofflaws who fail to keep current on their vehicle registrations. Then, when they're stopped, they expect the officer to take sympathy on them, and when they don't, they blame the officer when they're cited. I can't tell you how often I've asked, "How important can it be to you if you were willing to risk losing your license by driving like that?" And once again, don't open the gates to the tear ducts. Crying is just as likely to show the officer that you regret getting caught, not necessarily having committed the infraction.

Don't expect the officer to have any sympathy for you if you're stopped after committing a flagrant violation. You can try to blame it on him, but any good officer knows that it's the motorist who's earned the citation; the officer merely observed the violation.

> ☑ **Blue Light Bulletin:** If you do attempt an excuse, do it when the officer first approaches you. Once he goes back to his car, if he returns with a ticket, it's a done deal. If you want a break after you've scribbled your name on the ticket, you're going to have to get it from the judge.

The officer arrives at the site of a collision at the intersection of 12th Avenue and East Cherry Street on a bright summer day. The intersection runs through the Seattle University campus; several students and faculty have gathered around, but no one appears overly concerned. The officer laments the apathy; *Sad, especially on a university campus*, he thinks.

The officer sees only one car in the intersection, which has rolled over onto its roof. The officer runs over to the vehicle to assist any occupants, but finds the car empty. The officer emerges, confused, thinking perhaps the vehicle is an unreported stolen car and the suspects have already run off.

"Anybody see anything?" the officer asks the crowd. Two people point toward a man in a phone booth on the corner.

"He's the driver?" the officer asks.

The same people who were pointing nod, then turn and walk away.

The officer calls on his radio to get a tow truck to the scene, and requests other officers to assist with traffic control. He sees no injuries, no other cars apparently involved, and no property damage other than the inverted vehicle. The officer walks over to the phone booth and signals for the man to come over and speak with him. The motorist hangs up and strolls over to the officer as if he's got all day.

"Are you hurt, sir?"

"No. I was talking to my insurance company." He points a thumb back at the phone booth.

"Was there anyone else in the car with you?"

"No. I was telling the insurance lady what happened, that it wasn't my fault."

"Were there any other cars involved?"

"Nope. I didn't do anything wrong."

"Did you hit anything?"

"Just the curb, I think. It was just an accident."

The officer scratches his head. "So, what happened?"

"It wasn't my fault," the motorist says.

"I didn't ask you that; I asked you what happened. How'd you flip your car over?"

"Well, you're not going to believe this, Officer, but I just left the car wash up the hill back there, and my tires were still wet, and well, that's why my car flipped over. That happens, you know."

"You're right, sir."

"What? You've seen this before?"

"No. You said I wasn't going to believe you. Please wait here; I'll be right back."

Sometimes it's not even the motorist who makes the excuse:

In one instance I was investigating a collision involving a seventeen-year-old boy and his passenger, a buddy from school. It was remarkable that no one had been injured or killed. He'd lost control while driving around a sharp corner. He'd over-corrected, causing his car to drift across the street, glance off a parked car, careen back across the street up onto the sidewalk, and finally come to rest three inches from a five-foot-high brick retaining wall.

"What the heck were you thinking?" I asked the boy.

"I guess I wasn't. I must have taken the corner too fast," he said. His eyes were wide and his hands were shaking.

"Ya think? You're lucky no one was coming the other way, or someone would have ended up right there." I pointed to Lakeview Cemetery a half block away.

"I know," he lowered his head. "Can I call my dad?

"Yeah, that sounds like a good idea."

I collected all the necessary information and returned to my car. I was impressed the young man didn't try to make any excuses. He owned up to his stupidity and appeared to have taken the lesson seriously. While the facts amounted to a negligent or even reckless-driving criminal citation, having considered all factors involved, I used my discretion, based upon his attitude and his apparent contrition, to issue a lesser, nevertheless expensive, infraction.

And then Dad showed up. How could this father have raised a son who takes responsibility for his actions and doesn't make excuses, only to arrive at the scene armed with a bushel-full himself?

"Officer, are you going to issue my son a citation?" he asked.

"Yes, sir; when an officer investigates a collision in this state, he's mandated to find fault if it can be determined according to the rules of the road," I said.

"And you found my son at fault?"

"Yes, sir; fortunately, there was no one else involved."

"So, he came around the corner right there?" Dad asked, pointing down the street to a sharp corner bordered by a concrete barrier running along the outside of the curve.

"Yes, sir; that's where he lost control, struck that parked car right there, and came back across the street, nearly hitting this wall. You can see his skid mark there—it's about fifty feet—uphill."

"But Officer, there's something I don't understand; I don't see how it could be his fault." The father's face began to tighten.

"What do you mean, sir?"

"Well, there's no way anyone could come around the corner that fast with . . . out . . . losing . . . control," his words slowed to a drip. I could see the realization arrive as the stiffness left his face. "I'm sorry, Officer; now I get it."

I explained to him my enforcement decision and he thanked me for my leniency, promising that his son wouldn't be driving again without him until he was satisfied his son understood both his own driving limits, and the limitations of his vehicle.

In another similar incident, the boy's father reacted quite differently. Intending to teach his son a lesson, the father forced the boy to contest the ticket in court. That lesson, however, was as elusive to me as it seemed to be for the judge and for the boy's dad, not to mention the boy himself. The father hadn't done his son much good, but I have to at least give him credit for standing by his son in court, no matter how ineffective he may have been.

Balancing the good and the bad again:

I was patrolling through a popular city park where rough roads cut through the grounds like veins on a muscular forearm. I came around the corner just in time to observe a young man driving so fast toward me that his car fishtailed and the tires skidded off the pavement, losing traction and throwing dirt and gravel across a parking turnout into a dense thicket of holly. He corrected his track when he saw me and skidded before slowing his car.

I spun my car around, caught up to him, and stopped him. I walked up to his car and explained his violation to him as if it wasn't obvious. The boy wasn't exactly disrespectful, but it didn't seem to me that he thought what he'd done was a big deal.

No actual imminent danger existed, but considering the large concentration of pedestrian and bicycle traffic in the park at that time of day and the limited sight distances because of the winding roads, the potential for danger was high. He did not accept responsibility and was not contrite in the least. I cited him for exceeding reasonable speed. Since I was driving in the opposite direction and had no pace with which to articulate his exact speed, I used a code that allows me to articulate his excessive speed based upon other observations. And that was that—or so I thought.

I found myself defending the ticket in a courtroom, but it wasn't the driver who challenged the ticket—it was his father. I read my citation's narrative into the court record before a magistrate, from my position seated at a table next to the defendant and his father.

"Do you have anything to say in your defense, Mr. Sanchez?" The judge asked the young man. The kid looked at his father; his father shrugged his shoulders. The kid looked at the judge.

"Um, no, Your Honor," the kid said.

"Why are we here, young man?"

"I don't know." The kid looked at his father again.

"Sir, was this your idea?" the judge asked the father.

"Yes, Your Honor."

"Did you have something you wanted to say on your son's behalf?"

"Not really, Your Honor; I just don't think he should've gotten a ticket."

The judge turned back to the young Sanchez. "Mr. Sanchez, did the officer accurately describe your actions on that day?"

"Pretty much, yes," the kid said.

"Okay, I'm going to make my decision. Mr. Sanchez," the judge began, speaking to the father, "I'm not sure that bringing your son in here without a plan is going to have whatever effect you'd hoped for, or teach whatever lesson you'd intended to teach. I'd prefer you focus on teaching your son how to be a safe driver, okay?"

"Yes, Your Honor," the father answered.

"Mr. Sanchez, please stand." The boy stood.

"Mr. Sanchez, I find sufficient fact to find you guilty of this infraction. In fact, in reading the statute, it appears this traffic code was written precisely for what you did. I hope you realize how your driving can affect other people on the road. Please make arrangements to pay your fine with the clerk before leaving court today. Next."

> ☑ **Blue Light Bulletin:** As you can see, excuses come in all shapes and sizes, and even from people other than the driver. Most leave behind a stench. People come up with all kinds of excuses, some better than others, but none as good or as effective as the simple truth.

Here's one more—just for laughs.

"Sir, I stopped you for driving at forty-eight miles per hour in a twenty-mile-per-hour school zone, which is under construction and has children present. Is there any legal reason to explain your speed?" Officer Jonathan Q. Law asked.

"Officer?"

"Yes, sir."

"You just don't understand how a BMW drives."

"Excuse me?"

"Officer, a BMW is a high-performance car. You just can't drive these the same way you'd drive a regular car."

"Oh, really?"

"Yes; it's true. It can cause severe engine damage if you drive a BMW at too low RPMs, if your speed drops."

"Um-hmm?"

"I know you think I'm crazy, Officer. I don't expect you to understand, but it's true. Just call any BMW dealer, and he'll tell you all about it. Like I said, you just don't know how a 2001 BMW 740iL drives. I'll give you an example: What kind of car do you drive, Officer?"

The officer reached back, pulled his ticket book from his back pocket, and flipped it open to a virgin citation. "I drive a 2000 740iL—BMW," the officer said, swallowing his smirk. "Please be sure to press hard, sir—four copies."

Sometimes I swear the gods have nothing better to do than to set us humans up for their own entertainment. In the end, excuses are often pathetic, but on occasion can be quite humorous. Next, you'll see what happens when motorists take the art of the excuse to the next level.

What if none of my excuses work?

So you've given the officer your best stuff. You've given excuses, sniveled, and even shed a tear or two, and still nothing. The cop must be made of stone. What else could you try? Hey, what about the annual Police Officers' Charity Drive? Perhaps the officer would appreciate a "donation" to this (or another favorite) charity.

If you think this is a good idea, you need to get out more; you've been watching too much television. What you may think of as a *charitable donation*, the cop's gonna see as an attempt to bribe him. Bribery is not the best way to get off with a warning. Very few cops are willing to risk their careers by accepting what someone would be willing to pay to get off on a traffic ticket. (Hell, no! It would take way more money than that!)

But seriously folks, the only thing that will come of offering to make a donation in exchange for getting out of a ticket will be the certainty you *will* get that ticket, in addition to possible charges for offering an officer a bribe.

"I like it when they go, 'I know your chief.' I always ask, 'Do you know Heath Crossland?' They say, 'No,' and I say, 'Well, that's who you need to know to get out of this ticket.'"

—Officer H. Crossland, Lancaster Police Department,
Texas Traffic Division

CHAPTER 7

I Was Just on My Way to . . .

...And you thought you had it bad.

In this chapter . . .

- ☑ More outrageous excuses actually used
- ☑ Bicyclists, pedestrians, and motorists
- ☑ The real power of bicycle and motorcycle cops

I love this one. This tactic comes under the heading *Incredible—or Unbelievable—Coincidences*. I'll pull someone over for speeding, running a red light or a stop sign, or even for a simple expired registration, and the violator will look at me, face as straight as an eastern Washington freeway, and tell me they were just on their way to . . .

Officers Z. Smith and Q. Jones pull over a man for speeding and running a stop sign. As they walk up to the car, the man is engaged in a frantic conversation with his wife. As Z. Smith approaches the driver's window, the conversation inside the vehicle comes to an abrupt end.

"Hello, sir. The reason I stopped you is you were driving at forty-five miles per hour in a thirty-mile-per-hour zone, and you failed to stop for the stop sign back there at Union Street. Is there any legitimate reason you can give me for your speed—an emergency, maybe?" Officer Z. Smith asks with a smile.

"Oh yes, Officer," the man says, looking over at his nervous wife in the passenger seat. "It's my wife; I have to get her to the hospital."

"Why? What's wrong?" Smith asks, his smile fading.

"Nothing."

"What do you mean, nothing?"

"Oh, I thought you meant with me."

"No, with your wife, sir."

"Oh, she needs to get to the hospital."

"Yes, we've established that. What's wrong—with her?" the officer asks as he glances at the passenger who remains sitting rigid and stern, staring out her window.

"She has to see the doctor," the driver replies, lowering his voice and looking around. "Female stuff," he whispers.

Officer Q. Jones has worked with Smith for several years now. The look on Jones's face shows he's sensing what Smith already suspects, and Jones knows he's about to be treated to a cat-and-mouse show.

"I'll call for an ambulance," Smith says.

"No! Uh, no—thank you, we just need to get to the hospital."

"It's not an emergency then?"

"No, well, it is, but . . ." The man shifts in his seat, and his eyes dart about the car's interior.

"But it must be an emergency if you were speeding."

"Well, not exactly an emergency then, umm . . ." The man's breathing becomes uneven.

"More like—urgent, then," Smith baits the man.

"Yes! It's urgent; that's it."

"Okay—which hospital?"

"What do you mean?"

"Which hospital are you going to? There are several on the hill: HMC, Virginia Mason, Providence, Swedish?" says Smith.

"Uh, Swedish," the man says, relieved, and sensing his release, ticket-free, is imminent.

"Do you know where it is?"

"Yes."

"Where?"

"Umm, well, I don't know *exactly*, but I know the area it's in."

"Right—okay, then, why don't you follow us," Smith says, pointing up the street as he and his partner turn back toward their patrol car.

"Follow you? What for?"

"We want to make sure you get there okay, this being urgent and all. How you doing there, ma'am?" Smith ducks and glances into the car at the man's wife.

"I'm doing just great, Officer," she says, as she rolls her eyes and looks askance at her husband. If looks could kill. . .

The man follows the patrol car and finds a parking space near the hospital emergency entrance, but he remains seated in his car as they approach. The man rolls down his window.

"Thanks so much, officers. We'll be fine now; you can go," the man says, hoping to God Z. Smith and Q. Jones will finally stop helping him. But alas—

"Oh, it was nothing," Officer Smith begins. "Besides, I got a bunch of paperwork to catch up on and I like to park right there next to the ambulance ramp to write. Don't let us keep you; what did you say—oh yeah, it's urgent. Hey Quince, why don't you go get us a couple of lattes while I finish helping these nice people." Smith begins to dig into his pocket, but Jones waves him off.

"Don't worry about it, Zach; I got this one—it was worth it."
Jones's smile grows as he strides toward the latte cart.

I've arrested people who were just on their way downtown to take care of their warrant. I've arrested dopers who were just on their way to treatment. I've arrested thieves in possession of stolen property on their way to return the item to the owner. And directly related to our purposes, I've stopped people with expired driver's licenses, registrations, and insurance policies who were just on their way to—well, you know.

Since we haven't yet addressed traffic violations sans vehicle, now would be an appropriate time. This next story involves a pedestrian violation. Incidentally, the suggestions I've made regarding how not to behave during traffic stops apply equally as well when you get stopped for a violation on foot.

It's interesting how our perspectives change depending on whether we're on foot, on a bicycle, a motorcycle, or in a car:

I think it's accurate to say that all of the people who use the modes of transportation listed above are also pedestrians at times, just as the vast majority of bicycle and motorcycle riders drive cars much of the time. But while engaged in using one form of transportation, they often view those using another type as if they're vermin sent from hell to ruin their day. I've seen it, and I've been on both the giving and receiving ends of this sentiment.

While the cyclist feels he's doing something good and wholesome for himself and Mother Earth—using no fossil fuels, taking up less parking space, causing less damage to the roads, and enhancing his physical fitness—he's also doing one other thing: He's holding up traffic—and probably me.

From a motorist's perspective:

How many times have you been stuck in traffic behind a bicyclist who's traveling at 7 mph in a 30-mph zone, panniers bulging, and riding eight feet from the curb? Yeah, I've been there too. Do they have a legal right to do this? Technically, yes. Does it make it any less annoying? Officially, no.

More people riding bicycles means fewer people driving cars, right? Sure, but it also means more bikes impeding motor vehicle traffic and causing frustration, which can lead to road rage. (Don't worry; we'll get to that too.) This is the case especially when a cyclist decides to morph between being a vehicle and being a pedestrian as it suits him. He's in the roadway—now he's on the sidewalk—oh, back in the road again. I must admit to getting a chuckle when I see the Lance Armstrong–wannabes, colorful, tortured Lycra bulging at their waists, riding side by side while blocking the entire lane of travel as they desperately attempt to catch up to the peloton.

From a bicyclist's perspective:

Now, let's hop on a bicycle and see how the perspective changes. The cyclist is riding as carefully as he can, and he's on a designated bike route. Numerous signs validate this. Of course that doesn't stop motor vehicle commuters from feeling as if the road is all their own. The cyclist is riding as fast as he can, but he's riding in the center of the lane, holding up traffic for blocks. Why would he do this? Perhaps it's because the last time he rode close to the side, some idiot shot open the driver's door from their parked car and sent the cyclist hurling through inner space.

A brilliant idea—simply share the road:

Both cyclists and motorists share equal responsibility for the chaos that sometimes results when the two share the road. But keep one thing in mind: You're talking on average one or two hundred pounds of human and bicycle vs. over a ton of automobile. It's no contest; the cyclist can be perfectly in the right, but he can also be perfectly squished. If you're driving a motor vehicle, please remember that cyclists are extremely vulnerable and most of them will appreciate your being considerate of their limitations. And if you're riding a bicycle, please return the consideration: Lose the arrogance and allow cars to pass when you have the chance to move to the side. Sharing the road goes both ways.

Pedestrians are just as guilty:

Now let's get back to the pedestrian violation. Officers were on foot patrol in a high-crime area: thieves, dopers, hookers, gang-bangers . . . you name the crime, I'll show you the slime. (Oh man, that's good—gotta love that Jack Webb, *Dragnet* lingo.)

The officers had gotten a report from radio dispatch, which a good citizen had called in—a good, anonymous citizen—about a guy loitering to buy or sell drugs. The citizen had provided a good description for a change. The officers arrive in the area and see a guy matching the description, jaywalking.

> ☑ **Blue Light Bulletin:** Dumb Criminal Mistake #1—committing a minor traffic violation while engaged in criminal activity.

"Hey—come on over here," Officer H. Kickassinger directs the scofflaw.

"Who—me?" the man says, pointing to his own chest, his eyebrows stretching upward onto his forehead.

"Yeah, you; you're the only one in the street heading toward a DON'T WALK signal." The man strolls back over to the officers.

"You have any ID on you?" Officer Kickassinger asks.

"For what? What did I do?"

"For jaywalking; see that red DON'T WALK signal over there?" The officer points to the sign.

"Yeah. So what?"

"You can't cross when that's lit."

"I know."

"Then why'd you cross against it?"

"I didn't."

"Oh, give me a break. Let's see some ID."

The jaywalker pulls out his grimy, nylon tri-fold wallet and spreads it open wide, displaying its contents to the officers.

☑ **Blue Light Bulletin:** Dumb Criminal Mistake #2—being in plain view.

He pulls his driver's license from a slot in his wallet. Kick-assinger and his partner T. Hammimup can clearly see a driver's license belonging to a different person protruding from a slot in the jaywalker's wallet.

"What's that?" Kickassinger asks, pointing to the remaining license. Kickassinger takes Mr. Jaywalker's license and hands it to Hammimup to do a computer check for wants and warrants.

"That other license. You know it's illegal to possess someone else's driver's license, right?"

"He's a friend."

"Really."

"Yeah; in fact, I was just gonna call him. That's why I was crossing the street: I was gonna ask someone for some change so I could call my friend—umm—" Jaywalker is pathetic in his attempt to glance discreetly at the name on the license in Hammimup's hand—"Juan, to let him know I have his license."

"Okay, sounds reasonable; what's Juan's phone number?"

"I don't know. I was gonna look it up."

"What's Juan's last name?" the officer asks, flipping the license upside down against his own chest.

"I forget."

"Yeah right. You don't know Juan, do you?"

"No, Officer. I'm sorry; I lied."

"Okay; now, no more lying—got that?"

"Yes."

"All right, where did you get the license?"

"I found it."

The officer rolls his eyes.

"No—really, Officer; I was just going to put it in a mailbox."

Mr. Jaywalker becomes Mr. Criminal as his wallet falls open, spilling several credit cards, each displaying a different name. The officers arrest him. At the station they discover his dope, which, by the way, according to Mr. Criminal, had been left there by a friend who'd borrowed his pants.

Final observations:

Whether you're in a car, on a motorcycle, or on a trike; if you're on a bicycle, or even on foot, please give the officer a break. I once stopped a guy who told me he was on his way to the department of licensing to get his license renewed; it had been expired for six months. I shook my head and asked him what the odds of that were: Getting stopped at the exact moment you'd decided to take care of that nasty business. It had to be nine quadrillion to one—at least, I told him.

The driver looked at me with the smarmiest, oiliest, and most contemptuous expression I think I've ever seen. I looked him squarely in the eye and said, "Listen, you put yourself in my position; you listen to what you just said; would you believe you?"

He bowed his head and thought about it for a moment. His look of contempt disappeared as he said, "No. I guess I really wouldn't believe me either."

I know I shouldn't have, but I gave him a warning. I'd made my point, and his concession seemed sincere enough. If his contrition was legitimate, it might serve as a lesson for the future. I told him to get his license renewed immediately. Besides, chances were another officer would probably stop him before I ever saw him again, anyway.

YOUR ORAL WARNING:

"If a violator pulls over—to the right—right away, rolls down the window, and waits patiently with hands on the wheel and admits the error right away, there's a distinct chance that he or she will get a warning for an equipment or registration violation."

—Officer D. P. Reddick, Denver Police Department

CHAPTER 8

You Only Stopped Me Because . . .

"You only stopped me because I'm elderly!"
"No, Ma'am . . . I stopped you for driving the wrong way."

In this chapter . . .

☑ Tickets and race, gender, and ethnic issues

☑ Tickets and licenses and registrations

☑ Staying in your car for safety's sake

☑ **Blue Light Bulletin:** Contrary to popular belief, cops don't wake up in the morning thinking: Man, I can't wait to get to work today so I can screw with _____. (Fill in the blank with race, gender, ethnicity, sexual orientation, gender identification, lifestyle choice, sock color, or whatever you choose.)

The "You only stopped me because" complaint is so common that I can't even remember how many times I've heard it. It's also ironic that motorists with this attitude display the very thing they accuse the officer of doing.

Reality check:

In most instances, due to glare, observation angles, and poor lighting, the officer often can't determine if the motorist is from planet Earth, never mind what his or her physical attributes are.

I remember standing by with another officer who'd made a traffic stop in a criminally active neighborhood. I was watching the ill-tempered motorist so the officer could safely write her a ticket. The young woman's venomous drone had me wishing the officer could write faster. She proclaimed in a tirade why she'd been crowned "Supreme Queen of Universal Victimhood."

"You know," she said to me.

"I know what?" I asked.

"You know why he's writing me a ticket, don't you?"

"Um, yep."

"Why?"

"Because you almost hit that lady there in the crosswalk." I pointed to an old lady, inching her way toward us with her walker.

"Un-unh, no way," she said, dripping with self-justification. "He stopped me because I'm black."

"Really?"

"Oh yeah. I know it—he doesn't like me because I'm black."

After listening to her rambling on and watching her behavior for the past ten minutes, I know I shouldn't have, but—not being a big fan of *what I shouldn't have* . . .—I said, "How do you know *that's* the reason he doesn't like you?"

Probably didn't do the citing officer any favors, but I couldn't help myself. Fortunately, she finally signed the ticket and drove off, her whining still fully engaged before she'd realized the insult. I have to admit that the comment had been unintentional, but upon further reflection, I'm glad I said it.

●
●
●

If you're looking for racism, sexism, ageism, truckerism, gayism, bikerism, or whateverism, I guarantee you'll find it—it's a self-fulfilling pursuit:

The vast majority of cops in the vast majority of traffic stops, stop people because of what they *do*, not because of how they live or what they look like. Am I saying a person's race, sex, sock color, or whatever, never plays a part in the officer's decision to cite once the person is stopped? No. I'd be disingenuous to deny this happens on occasion. However, every human being, consciously and subconsciously, uses diverse factors that will determine how he reacts to or treats his fellow man. Some people are just plain jerks. No, really. Trust me on that.

Just like using the first words out of your mouth to call the cop a liar isn't the best idea, calling the cop a racist or a sexist without provocation isn't likely to move you to the top of the warning list either.

I once got behind a pretty college-age girl driving a bright, shiny red Mazda Miata convertible with the top down. The girl was driving uphill at 45 mph in a 30-mph zone, and approaching a curve around which a school zone ran for two blocks. Fifteen over the limit, in a residential neighborhood, approaching a school zone: Yeah, that's worth at least a stop and a chat. My inclination at that point was to give her a warning, so long as she had a decent attitude and didn't have any outstanding tickets or a poor driving record.

"Why did you stop me?" she asked, before I'd even made it up to her window. The indignant brunette didn't even turn her head toward me.

"Good morning," I greeted her in a friendly tone, in an attempt to bring the encounter back to civility, and for her sake, into the realm of an oral warning.

"I asked you why you stopped me?" She turned slowly toward me this time. Oops—she'd all but already earned herself a ticket, but hey, it was a nice day and I was in a good mood.

"Has a police officer ever done something to make you this angry?"

"Yeah, you."

"You don't even know why I stopped you yet."

"Oh, I know why you stopped me."

"Really? Why?"

"Because you probably always stop cute girls driving red convertible Miatas."

You know, you never have the right comeback in situations like that, because they're so unbelievable they take you by surprise. On retrospect, I should have told her she was wrong, and said, "No, I'll stop *any* girl driving a red convertible Miata."

Don't think I don't know how contrived this story sounds; I do, but I assure you, it happened. As I said at the beginning of this book, all the anecdotes are based upon actual events that happened to me, or that my fellow officers reported back to me. Some stories are composites of various incidents, which I use to illustrate my points and to save time. The accuracy of some of the peripheral details of these anecdotes isn't as important as the lessons they teach. However, there is nothing better than police work to prove the old adage: Truth *is* stranger than fiction.

Oh, I forgot—yeah, she had to press hard—four copies.

On another occasion, I was on routine patrol and I observed a car up ahead displaying expired registration tabs, three months overdue. Although it's an infraction to display expired tabs even if the vehicle registration is actually current, I normally choose not to stop a vehicle until I have verified with my computer that the registration is valid. The computer Department of Licensing (DOL) records confirmed the vehicle registration was three months expired.

"Hello, ma'am. The reason I stopped you is because it appears your license registration tabs have expired. They show April 2000."

"Oh, that couldn't be, Officer."

"I assure you it is, ma'am," I said.

At this point the driver invariably wants to get out and look at the tabs. It's as if she thinks the tabs will magically change when she checks them. Even though I've been behind her for several blocks, verified the expiration with my computer, and visually confirmed it as I approached the car, she believes her registration will have somehow been renewed through some registration alchemy in the few moments since I first approached her car.

We always take safety precautions—always:

I ask most folks to remain in their car for safety reasons, both for the violator and for me. In heavy traffic it can be dangerous to walk around your car. On other occasions, if there is little threat from the motorist or from passing traffic, I'll allow the driver to get out and see it with her own eyes. I must admit to having an ulterior motive here. Coppin' can get boring on some days, and the entertainment value in watching the motorists' faces contort as they stare at their expired registrations is priceless.

"But I never got a notice to renew it in the mail," she says.

"The state issues those as a courtesy, ma'am. It's your responsibility to remember."

"Can I get out and see for myself?"

"You don't believe me?"

"Oh no, it's not that, Officer—it's just—well, they can't be expired."

"I assure you they are, ma'am, but if it'll make you feel better, have at it."

"What?"

"Go ahead and check."

She gets out and strolls to the back of the car with a puzzled look on her face. She rubs her chin, combs her fingers through her hair, and then looks at the ground for a moment. "Well, huh—I wonder how that happened? I thought they were up-to-date. You know, the state really should send something."

"Yes, ma'am. Please sign here."

Sometimes even stops for the simplest infractions can be harrowing for an officer:

It was dusk, and I was driving behind a nondescript minivan with tinted windows. I couldn't see how many occupants might be in the vehicle, but had to assume there was at least a driver (remote-controlled vans on the roads being so rare these days). I verified in my computer that the registration was indeed expired. It had expired in June, and it was now August.

I activated my lights and the van pulled to the side, just past a busy intersection. I walked up to the driver's door and met only my own reflection staring back at me in the tinted window. After taking a moment to admire myself in my crisp uniform, I tapped on the window. I stepped toward the rear, past the door's swing area, and asked, "Could you roll down the window, please?" It's eerie wondering if the person on the other side of the glass has just committed some crime and is pointing a gun at you. (Improbable, perhaps, but it does happen.)

Again, I saw only me staring back. "Please roll down the window," I said with greater emphasis, tapping on the window and trying to project my authority through the window. It must have worked, because the window began to slowly slide down. When it had traveled about an inch, it stopped. I could now see that the driver appeared to be a middle-aged, professional-looking woman.

"Ma'am, could you please roll down your window a tad further?"

"This'll be just fine. You told me to roll it down, and it's down. Now, what do you want?"

"Ma'am, the reason I stopped you is because your tabs are expired."

The woman lowered the window another half an inch and looked at me with hard eyes. "The reason you stopped me is because I'm a woman," she said.

"Ma'am, your van has tinted windows. I couldn't even see your gender or age, never mind your race before I stopped you."

"Whatever—get on with it—you're gonna ticket me anyway."

"Ma'am, you're going to have to open the window a bit more so I can slip this in for you to sign." I lifted my ticket book toward her. It was obvious that my book was too thick to fit through the slot.

She launched herself into such a tirade I can barely recall a single separate word. They all jumbled together into one giant ream-out session. When she stopped talking she was actually winded. She provided her license and registration, slipping the documents through the narrow slot. I went back to my car and completed the citation, returning to the van. She'd given me no reason to issue a warning. The window remained open, barely an inch and a half.

"Are you finished?" I asked.

The woman said nothing; she just sat there, breathing heavily. I figured I couldn't be the sole source of her misery and kind of felt sorry for her.

"Please roll down your window some more." The woman lowered the window with a sigh.

"Okay then, I just need to get your signature here, by signing this—"

"Here; that's what you want, always out here harassing good neighborhood folks—here—" she said, snatching the ticket book and pen from me. After signing the ticket, she shoved my ticket book and pen back into my chest.

"Are there any questions I can—" I began to ask as she ignored me and shifted her van into gear. She rocketed forward before I'd even had a chance to move away from the vehicle; I barely had time to snatch my foot away from her rear wheel's path.

I dashed back to my patrol car and took off after her. I caught up with her five blocks down the road.

"What now?" she asked, incensed.

"What now?" I said. "You nearly ran over my foot back there."

"Oh, you're just harassing me because I'm a strong black woman."

"No, ma'am, I'm stopping you this time because you almost ran over a police officer's foot—mine! Please wait right here."

I called for a backup unit and returned to my car to write her another citation, this time a criminal ticket for negligent driving. Some drivers are their own worst enemies; don't you be.

What you see is what you get:

This driver was looking for racism, or sexism, or both—and guess what? She found it. It's not hard to find something when a person creates his own definition for it. Hypersensitive people of all descriptions will find the discrimination they seek, because they enter into any encounter that displeases them with prejudiced preconditions. There's the fat person who finds fat discrimination, the biker who sees people who don't like bikers everywhere, and the gay person who finds homophobia everywhere he looks. Bad service at a hotel: It's because I'm a biker. Waitress gave bad service: It's because I'm gay. Loan didn't get approved: It's because I'm Southeast Asian and German-Polish on my mother's side and Lithuanian, Korean, and Cherokee on my father's side. Come on; *give me a break!*

The plain ol' truth:

The officer stopped you because you were speeding, you ran the red light, or you almost ran over that Buddhist nun in the cross-walk—not because of how you look, think, feel, or pray. You were stopped because of your actions. Now get over it; the world's not out to get you—you're not as important as you think you are.

So what do you suppose is the one seemingly innocuous thing a motorist can do to guarantee he'll get a ticket instead of a warning? To the motorist, it might seem like the prudent act of an important person, but to the officer, it's the impudent act of a jackass. Read on to find out.

YOUR ORAL WARNING:

"One blonde I stopped, when asked if she'd noticed the red light she had just gone through, told me: 'I'm not from around here.' I asked her if they had red lights where she was from."

—Officer B. Peters, Pittsburg, Kansas

CHAPTER 9

Talk to My Lawyer

"Oh yeah? Why don't you just talk to my lawyer . . ."

In this chapter . . .

☑ Lawyers are not intimidating to cops

☑ Big egos equal big tickets

☑ Lawyers tend to give the same advice cops give

"The first thing we do, kill all the lawyers." Dick, the butcher, posits this proposal in Shakespeare's *Henry VI*. After several centuries this remains a popular sentiment. While I appreciate the quote and sometimes think it might be worth considering, I have to admit that I know too many lawyers who probably shouldn't be killed; I imagine that being a lawyer in today's society is, at times, punishment enough.

There's this strange dichotomy of reaction when someone introduces themselves as a lawyer. One reaction is admiration, but it rarely stands alone; it's usually accompanied by one of several companion emotions, including intimidation, fear, and in some cases, disgust. A lot depends on your point of view. As a cop, I'd amend the quote to read, "kill all the *defense* lawyers." Of course, if I were to be accused of a crime myself, I'd immediately regret my edict.

To be effective, a lawyer need not be palatable to civil society. I have a former firefighter/bar owner/motorcycle buddy whose bar burned down—twice. I asked him how things were going, and he said that he had his lawyer working on the details. I asked him if his lawyer was any good.

This is essentially how my friend described his attorney: *My lawyer is an absolute flaming scumbag. I feel sick to my stomach just speaking with him on the phone; in fact, I'm getting a little queasy just thinking about him right now. He's so slimy I won't even go to his office or meet with him in person anywhere for fear I'll be struck down by a lightning bolt. I certainly wouldn't allow him into my house or business because I wouldn't want to expose my customers, friends, or family to such a subhuman wretch. In other words, yeah, you bet—he's a damn good lawyer.*

As you can see, lawyers are a lot of things; they run the gamut and spectrum of many lists. However, being intimidating to cops is not normally one of those things. I'm not quite sure what lurks deep inside a pea-brained motorist that would make him think a police officer would be threatened by a lawyer. An officer learns early on that there is nothing about a lawyer, with few exceptions, that makes him the least bit intimidating.

Just to show I'm not going to pick solely on defense attorneys, I can remember years ago sitting on the stand in court, a witness for the city, represented by a dimwitted prosecutor. I had to use my well-honed telepathic gifts to try to get her to object at an obvious time during the defense examination. My acute telepathic skills involved intense staring, a great deal of throat clearing, and significant raising of eyebrows, until the lawyer finally got my point and objected. The funny thing is, the judge's stare had been as intense as mine, and I could swear he'd engaged his own telepathy as well. Impressive? Intimidating? Not really.

To be fair, I'm sure prosecutors deal with their share of not-so-bright officers on the stand as well, but that's not part of our discussion for right now, is it? So all you lawyers can calm down and we'll get back to the issue at hand. I've stopped a lawyer or two in my day, and I can tell you one thing: You folks could use this information as much as anyone else.

That's why it baffles me to no end when, on a stop, violators want to call their lawyers in an obvious attempt to intimidate me into giving them warnings. I just tell 'em to go right ahead and talk their hearts out. I then return to my patrol car to scribble out a citation. When I get back to the violator's car, I tell 'em to hang up the phone so they can sign their ticket. The funny thing is, I've also had lawyers call their lawyers. Shouldn't they know better?

On one particular stop I pulled over a man for running a stop sign. He was in his thirties and was driving a bright yellow late-model sports car—I think it was a Honda Del Sol. The man wore material success like a badge, and whether he was more obnoxious or cocky was anyone's guess. His arrogance and attempt to intimidate me were impressive; impotent, but impressive nonetheless.

I approached the car. As I got to the door he rolled down his window without saying a word and handed me his cell phone. (In case you're wondering, and at the risk of losing the suspense, I decided to write him right then, regardless of whatever else he said or did—even if he happened to be the police chief's favorite dog walker, he was getting a ticket—for sure.)

I took the phone and looked at him quizzically. He said, "Talk to my lawyer."

I looked at the phone and then back at him and then back at the phone. I pressed the END button, disconnecting the phone call.

I requested and received his driver's license, registration, and insurance card, handed the phone back to him, and said, "Wait here; I'll be right back." I returned with a ticket in need of his signature. As expensive as the ticket was, the amount of the fine still didn't come close to equaling the amount of ego that guy had. Still, he didn't have to get a ticket. This was a stop for which I routinely issue warnings, but since he went through all that effort to get a ticket, obliging him was the least I could do.

I'm not sure what compels some people to do the exact opposite of what would be in their best interest in a given circumstance. We police officers often discuss common sense amongst ourselves. Many officers have come to believe that common sense is more myth than fact with a lot of the motorists we stop. How we make our own decisions is in large part based upon common sense, and a lot of our job security is due to a lack of it.

☑ **Blue Light Bulletin:** Common sense dictates that in order to nuzzle your way into someone's good graces, when attempting to acquire a particular objective, one should treat a potential benefactor with kindness and respect.

One would *think* that would be the obvious thing to do. Instead, some folks decide the best way to cajole their way into the potential benefactor's good graces is through disrespect and intimidation; in other words, by utterly disregarding common sense.

Common sense also dictates that even a mediocre lawyer is going to give his client advice based not upon an ego battle at the scene, but based upon what would be best for his client in the courtroom. Each motorist I've stopped who has decided to call his attorney has had one thing in common with the next guy: The lawyer has advised them to do exactly as I say. With few exceptions, each motorist has received a citation that could have been a warning instead, had they chosen to conduct themselves in a civil manner.

After the Del Sol driver did everything possible to talk himself into multiple citations, he wasn't finished yet. Now he was about to talk his way from a simple traffic infraction into jail. I returned to his car with the completed citation. (In my jurisdiction, I can write up to three violations on one ticket.)

"Okay, sir, I just need to get your signature and you'll be on your way. By signing this citation, you're not admitting to any guilt; you're simply agreeing to comply with the instructions on the back of your copy of the citation. You'll have three options for handling the ticket: You can pay it; you can request a mitigation hearing to explain the circumstances; or you can contest the infraction. Make your decision and send it in within fifteen days. Do you have any questions?"

"I'm not signing that."

"Why not?"

"Because I didn't do anything wrong."

"Sir, I just explained you're not admitting any guilt. You can see right below the signature line here; it reads that you're not admitting you committed the infractions—just that you received the ticket and will respond as directed in your instructions."

"I'm not signing that."

"Sir—do you know that by failing to sign, you would be committing a crime for which you could go to jail?"

"No way."

"I'm afraid so; will you sign now?"

"No."

"You're kidding me, right? You'd rather go to jail for the weekend?"

"I'd really go to jail if I don't sign?"

"Yes. I'd have to call out a sergeant who would explain what I've just explained to you, and if you still refuse to sign, I will arrest you and put you in jail."

He sat thinking about it for a moment, then turned to me and asked, "Can I call my lawyer?"

I sighed loudly, but thought that might be better than having to call my sergeant away from Starbucks (I mean, his office). "What the heck—go ahead," I said. I knew what the lawyer would say.

I heard mumbling on the phone from within the vehicle, through the closed windows. I caught, "Are you sure?" and "You're kidding me." He ended the call and rolled down his window. Without a word and without looking at me, he held his hands out for the ticket book and pen. He signed the ticket with such a violent flourish he nearly tore the paper. I decided not to make a big deal out of the continued disrespect. Like a hangover, he'd regret it in the morning.

I provided him with his copy, and as I was asking him if he had any questions, he drove off in an impressive huff, although I knew he was dying to squeal those tires to give me a true representation of what he thought about me, the stop, and every single cop on the face of the Earth. I glanced up the road as the vehicle faded into the distance, and waved. *Drive safely*, I said in my head.

Now, it's bad enough when a motorist threatens to call his attorney during a stop, or actually does so; but what am I supposed to think when it's a lawyer I've stopped, and he acts in a similar manner?

"Do you know who I am?" the well-dressed young man said to me as I arrived at his car window.

"Maybe. According to your registration information in my computer . . . you're Chadwick W. Moorehead," I said.

"Yes, that's me; but that's not what I meant."

"Oh; what did you mean, then?"

"I'm somebody, you know?"

"Yes, I'm sure you are, sir; in fact, I was kind of counting on that when I first saw your car driving down the street."

"No! You're just making fun of me and I don't appreciate it. This is not coming out right at all."

"Why don't you start over again, sir?"

"You don't have to be a smartass."

"I'm sorry if you think that, sir. I'm just waiting for you to inform me as to who you are that might make a difference to me in this stop."

"I'm an attorney," he said, having finally purged himself of a revelation he'd obviously thought was self-evident.

"Congratulations, sir; your parents must be so proud. Could I please see your driver's license, registration, and proof of current insurance?"

"Doesn't that mean anything to you, Officer?"

" . . . What difference does it make to me if you're a lawyer, an astronaut, or an Iowa corn inspector? Perhaps if you were the chief of police, that might—*might*—make a difference. Your occupation doesn't change the fact that you ran a red light."

"I'll fight the ticket. I know how the court system works, you know."

"I seriously doubt that, sir. If you did, you wouldn't be saying all of these things that I'll be writing in my ticket narrative for the judge to read."

"The judge is going to read what I said?"

"Of course; I wouldn't want to deprive the court of your side of the story, sir." The young lawyer sat stewing for a moment, apparently boggled by the fact his comments would be used against him in a court of law, before he took a deep breath and spoke again.

"Can we just get this over with?" the man asked.

His terse, but calm, request was an obvious sign that the young lawyer at least remembered something from law school, like, words have power. They can be used to build a case up or tear one down. They can also come back to help or haunt you.

"Sure; I just need to get your signature here. Please press hard, sir—four copies."

He took the ticket book. I think he might have even smiled, but it might have been a bit of indigestion. He signed the ticket with a pretentious flourish.

"Thank you, sir. Oh, and by the way—just how long have you been a lawyer anyway?" I asked.

"Never mind!" he said, his car's tires chirping ever so slightly as he drove away. His shiny graduation tassel swung happily from his rearview mirror.

YOUR ORAL WARNING:

"What [makes me most mad] is when, prior to the contact, [drivers] are on a cell phone, yelling back at me, 'Why did you stop me?' The basic rule of thumb is, treat me badly and there is no way you're driving off without a ticket."

—Officer H. Crossland, Lancaster Police Department, Texas, Traffic Division

CHAPTER 10

Only Hot Chicks Get Warnings

"You only pulled me over because I'm hot!"
"Trust me, Ma'am, that's not the case."

In this chapter . . .

☑ Beauty is in the eye of the beholder

☑ Attitude weighs more heavily than looks do

☑ The attitude test

First of all, I'm toying with you a bit by using this titillating, provocative, and perhaps a bit gratuitous chapter title. (I'm so ashamed.) However, this phenomenon is no myth.

> ☑ **Blue Light Bulletin:** Attractive people may indeed have a better chance at getting a warning instead of a ticket. However, there is something that levels the playing field: We have to consider what makes one person attractive to another person, and it isn't always appearance. It is, after all, a subjective matter.

For instance, I might look at an actress like Catherine Zeta-Jones and think, *Wow!* Conversely, I may have a buddy who looks at her and says, incredibly, "What's the big deal?" (Oh yeah; if I stop her, you bet she's getting a warning. I don't care if she was doing 90 in a 30, in a rainstorm, at night, with her headlights off, blindfolded, through a school zone under construction; yes—she's getting off with a warning.)

But seriously folks, I'm going to delve deeper into the issue than the title may imply. You may recall a *Seinfeld* episode in which Jerry is dating a gorgeous blonde. As the episode progresses, we see the pretty woman getting special service by everyone around her—basically being treated as if she were Helen of Troy. And in the end, to top things off, we're shown the coup de grâce: a traffic stop.

Jerry sees the cop's lights in his rearview mirror, pulls his car to the side of the road, and stops. He exudes an obnoxious confidence with his beautiful date sitting beside him. The officer walks up to Jerry's car and asks him if he knows how fast he was going. Jerry acts unconcerned and says he has no idea. The officer tells him his speed. Jerry responds with something like, *I thought I was going much faster than that, Officer; you should have seen me a few miles back—man, I was really flying.* The officer is not amused and is all set to slap paper on Jerry, when Jerry cues his girlfriend to get out of the car to *encourage* the officer to reconsider. Did it work? You bet it did. It's TV after all—just fiction. *Yeah, right.*

Beauty is subjective:

My wife is fond of the eloquent aphorism, "Men are pigs." It's probably true, but it's not my point in this instance. It's well known that people respond to the attractive differently than they do to the unattractive. However, beauty is subjective; what makes a person attractive to one may make her unattractive to another. The way I figure it, the breaks get shared around. All else being equal, different officers will give breaks to different violators for different reasons, based upon multiple factors of which appearance may be one.

This is not to say the person is getting a warning *because* they're attractive; I'm just saying that in some instances, it doesn't hurt if an officer finds you attractive for whatever reason. I'm thinking about the borderline cases where one of those curve-balls waggles up my secret formula. In those cases (even if sub-consciously), the officer might tilt toward a warning—but that's just human nature.

> ☑ **Blue Light Bulletin:** What matters a lot more than looks, however, is attitude.

Pay attention, you're being tested:

When the officer approaches you, after noting visual cues, the first thing he does is give you an attitude test. You may not even know you're taking it, and the rookie officer might not even be aware he's giving it, but take my word for it; you are, he is, and it behooves you to pass it. It only takes a second to pass or fail this test. Your demeanor and how you initially address the officer can have a significant impact on whether you get off with a warning or receive a citation.

Some years ago my partner and I were patrolling on Capitol Hill one quiet, sunny day. It was my partner's day to drive, and my day *on paper*—meaning, writing reports. He observed a flagrant stop-sign violation, chased the car down, and stopped it. The violator was a stunning, raven-haired beauty wearing dark sunglasses and driving a red sports car—a Mitsubishi 3000GT, if I remember correctly. You've got to trust me on this; this woman was supermodel-hot, as if she'd just slipped off the cover of *Maxim* magazine. She pulled to the side of the road. My partner, who was probably thinking this was his lucky day, approached her vehicle. The woman surprised him with a seductive Italian accent, but before he was able to ask for her license, this beautiful European flower launched into a tirade the likes of which have rarely been heard or seen on either side of the Atlantic, or for that matter, the Pacific and Indian Oceans as well.

I mean, she was *crazy*. She screeched at the top of her lungs and called my partner every name under the Tuscan sun, mostly in distorted English, but sprinkled with the occasional Italian invective. Her barrage was relentless. He was a "this" and he was a "that," and then he was a "this" and a "that" combined—well, you get the idea. My partner returned to the patrol car, his pre-conceived image shattered. Chalk it up to a mischievous god tossing up another one of those curveballs.

"What are you going to do?" I asked.

"I don't know; maybe I should write her."

(Like my wife says, men are indeed pigs.)

"*Maybe?* Why are you hesitating—you think you'll be going out with her anytime soon?" I asked. "Good point," he said as he snatched up his ticket book.

To be honest, I thought about this phenomenon when I was a rookie. I thought about it and knew I didn't want to have such inconsequential things as a motorist's looks influence me—for good or bad. So, what did I do? I leapt to the other extreme. I once stopped a young woman driving a Jeep Wrangler for expired registration. Not only was she attractive, she was also quite pleasant.

I was inclined to give her a warning and give her time to get the renewal; the registration had been expired for just two days past my normal discretionary grace period. Immediately I began thinking I'd give her a warning instead of a citation because I found her attractive. To confront and refute this inclination, I issued the poor girl a ticket. In retrospect, it didn't bother me in an ethical way; her car was two weeks expired, and she legitimately warranted a citation. However, it affected me more on a human level. As my experience grew, I accepted the person as a whole and acted according to the law, to department policy, and to my principles, out of which eventually came my "secret formula." If a woman is cute, then bonus for me: Who doesn't enjoy a conversation with a pleasant person whom they consider attractive, and who might not otherwise give them the time of day? But what the heck—my wife doesn't let me date much anyway.

As human beings, our interactions with one another will always be affected by certain influences, whether consciously or subconsciously. We won't always realize it at the time. We might have immediate sympathy for a particular person, feeling some sort of innate kinship, and not immediately recall the time in our past when a similar person in some way once helped us out or showed us some kindness. This is natural and is not necessarily a bad thing. Again, these breaks get shared around.

The officer who does give breaks to people based upon a predetermined subjective influence—such as physical appearance, regardless of other contributing circumstances—is in my opinion behaving dishonorably and is guilty of allowing himself to be manipulated by the motorist. Generally in law enforcement, it's never in the officer's best interest to give away power. If an officer lets someone off exclusively because of one reason, such as good looks, he's given his power away—he's been played.

Does the officer believe that the blonde in the convertible would actually give him the time of day if she wasn't interested in getting out of a ticket? Hell no! I'm not saying that it doesn't happen from time to time that a social arrangement might be forthcoming from such an interaction, but I'd submit that they are so extremely rare as to be not worth the risk of compromising your integrity. Besides, after the stop, while you're busy looking like an idiot admiring yourself in your rearview mirror, you'll already be forgotten by the pretty blonde as she speeds off toward her next encounter down the road with the next easily manipulated officer.

If your good looks and/or nice personality get you a break from a cop here and there—well, good for you:

On your end of the equation, who cares what the reason is—right? Again, regardless of your looks and pleasant personality, *just be honest.* I can't emphasize this point enough, and you'll hear me bring this up time and again, because it's critically important in an encounter with the police.

For example: Last night I was watching a local evening magazine show with my wife. The show was doing their annual "Best and Worst of" show: best bed-and-breakfast . . . best-looking police officer (yes, really—and yes, she was cute) . . . worst speed trap, etc.

For the segment they watched a trooper as he ran radar on this relatively short corridor between Seattle and Tacoma on I-5. Apparently this stretch of road has won the speed trap award for four straight years, and as the trooper commented, "I guess these drivers just don't learn." The host interviewed two or three of those stopped who agreed to talk to him. They were in good spirits and understood they'd been stopped for speeding. One guy had been stopped for 76 mph in a 60-mph zone. His excuse: His mother had told him that 10 mph over the limit was okay. Regardless; he was 16 mph over the limit, not to mention 6 mph over his mother's advised limit. When the host asked the trooper what he thought about the mother's advice, the trooper responded, "The speed limit is the speed limit." Nothing ambiguous about that.

One girl from Oregon turned the tables on the cop with regard to this chapter's title. When interviewed by the TV show's host, she simply stated (about the officer), "Well, at least he's cute."

As the segment came to a close, I received yet another confirmation from the universe about why a book such as this one is so badly needed. The host asked the trooper what kind of driver's excuses work best with him. As if on a cue from me, his answer was, "No excuse—just tell the truth. So many people lie that when a driver admits they were speeding and apologizes, it shocks me. Heck, a lot of times I let those people go." I really hope you're paying attention.

So what if attractive people get more breaks? From my perspective, the more pleasant the person, the more attractive they appear. Do you think my partner finds Ms. Italiano attractive now? Me neither. And don't expect to use your looks either.

> ☑ **Blue Light Bulletin:** You may run into that one cop who sees it as an affront and who becomes more inclined to write you specifically because you're flaunting whatever you feel passes for your good looks.

YOUR ORAL WARNING:

"What the traffic violator doesn't understand is that we start out the contact with an arm's length of discretion, but when they start running off at the gums, that discretion shrinks to the point of a needle."
—Detective R. Smith, Seattle Police Department

CHAPTER 11

I've Been Driving Since Before You Were Born!

"I don't see the problem, Officer."
"I didn't think you did."

In this chapter . . .

☑ Acknowledging deteriorating driving skills

☑ Retaking driving tests

☑ We'll all be "Sunday drivers" someday

The date of birth on his driver's license read: 11/03/98. I blinked several times and read it again. Eleven—zero-three—ninety-eight. I first thought it was a misprint, but was stunned when I finally realized the driver was born in 1898. When I became a cop in 1992, I never imagined I'd stop someone who'd been born in the previous century.

I checked his driving record; it was spotless for at least the past five years (a miniscule percentage of his entire time on the road, I realized). I hadn't even stopped him for a moving violation; the registration tabs on his license plates were expired. For some reason, I couldn't shake that encounter out of my mind.

When it was suggested I include a chapter specifically dealing with the concerns of more mature drivers, I was at a loss. I thought the advice in this book pretty much fit all drivers, regardless of age. While this is true, after I thought about it and discussed the idea with my former patrol partner, I realized that age-specific advice might benefit older drivers—and most of us will eventually be in that category.

Becoming a danger on the road:

Let's begin with a serious issue. I run into lots of poor drivers. Most poor driving I see has nothing to do with the motorist's age, whether it be youthful inexperience or age-related mental or physical decline. However, on occasion I do run into a case of an elderly driver whose driving skills have deteriorated to the point where they become a danger to other drivers on the road. This brings us to a very sensitive question: When is it time to hang up the car keys? Some of us will maintain safe driving skills up until the last day we park the car in the garage, go to bed that night, and fail to wake in the morning. Not all of us will be so lucky.

As we become older drivers, we're more likely to have impaired hearing and vision, slower reflexes, and less range of motion and muscle strength—making it more difficult to look back over our shoulder for traffic—and thus making us dependent on less-reliable rear- and side-view mirrors. As our eyesight deteriorates, we need more light to see well. Our eyes become more sensitive to glare and our peripheral vision narrows. If we use eyedrops, they can cause our vision to become blurry.

One way to mitigate these issues is to gain a bit more reaction time by increasing following distances. For instance, if you use the traditional two-second rule, meaning you'll pass the point the car ahead of you passed two seconds later, then increasing your distance to three seconds will reduce your chances of a collision and a ticket.

Another way to decrease the likelihood of getting into a colli-sion—or getting stopped by the police for traditional age-related infractions, such as failing to yield to oncoming traffic, com-pletely stopping at a stop sign, or driving through a red light—is to use your common sense and avoid driving when it's more dan-gerous for you. This might mean curtailing your night driving, not driving in inclement weather, and avoiding driving on higher-speed highways and freeways.

Another consideration is if you're involved in multiple colli-sions and are receiving too many traffic tickets, your insurance company may refuse to renew your policy. But there is a way you can fight back, hold on to the freedom and independence your car provides, and continue to drive—albeit more safely. I'm talking about taking a defensive-driving course. By participating in one of these courses, you may even turn the tables on your insurance company and instead of paying them more money or losing your coverage altogether, you could actually save yourself some cash by qualifying for a rate reduction. Some insurance companies offer discounts to drivers who successfully complete these courses. Courses are available for both automobile and motor-cycle operators.

There are several defensive-driving courses out there, and some have a specific focus on older drivers. The American Asso-ciation of Retired Persons (AARP), for example, has been operat-ing a defensive-driver refresher course since 1969. In 1979 the program became known as AARP 55ALIVE Driver Safety Program when it added specific training for age-related cognitive and physical changes most drivers experience as they grow older. AARP reports that nine million people have taken the course since 1969, and 700,000 people now take the course annually. I like the course because it continually updates its training curricu-lum every few years, keeping it fresh and relevant.

There is no actual driving involved in the eight-hour course, and those of you who haven't shaken your test anxiety since your school days needn't worry; there is no test. This valuable information and useful tips are designed for you to integrate into your driving. You see it or read it and then simply apply it to your own driving. The proof of its effectiveness is in the results.

A new development at 55ALIVE is the addition of an online version of their driver safety course. The online course offers the same curriculum as in the classroom, but in the comfort of your own home. The online course is now available nationwide at: http://www.aarp.org/families/driver_safety/driver_safety_online _course.html.

The American Automobile Association (AAA) also offers driver's resources in the form of informative pamphlets, which can be downloaded and printed from a home computer. The AAA site also offers a video library with video clips offering driving tips. A list of alternative transportation resources is also provided for those who wish to reduce their time behind the wheel.

To register for a course or to find more information, you can visit www.aarp.org on the Internet, or you can contact your state AARP office. You can find the AAA website at www.seniordrivers .org. Phone numbers for their national and local offices can be found in your phone book.

For those of you who are interested in a more hands-on approach, there are plenty of driver-education companies out there who'd be more than happy to take your money, and you, for a few spins around the block. However, don't assume they're going to treat you any differently than the new sixteen-year-old driver. I'd suggest you ask specific questions about their knowl- edge and integration of age-related driving concerns in their cur- riculum and if they specifically offer actual refresher courses.

Statistics have shown that drivers who've taken the 55ALIVE refresher course have experienced reduced collisions and viola- tions. They also report taking the course has caused them to change the way they drive for the better. As a cop this doesn't sur- prise me. Many of us who've been driving for many years have developed bad habits; sometimes we just need to have them pointed out to us and be given an explanation as to what makes some driving habits bad, for us to make the necessary corrections. Hell, some older drivers got their licenses before organized driving instruction existed. It was some of these folks who taught their own kids to drive and likely passed along bad habits they'd developed over the years.

I remember one buddy from high school that learned to drive a year before I did. His father didn't want to pay good money for someone else to teach his son something he was *perfectly capable of teaching himself.*

One day my buddy snuck out in his parents' car before he'd actually gotten his license and took me for a drive. Now I wasn't a licensed driver either, but I was still awestruck when I saw he drove the car using both feet. No, the car didn't have a manual transmission; it was an automatic. He drove with his right foot on the gas pedal and his left foot on the brake pedal. I asked him why he was driving with both feet and told him I'd never seen anyone drive like that before. He told me his father had taught him to do it that way. I'll tell you what, his sympathy reflexes played havoc with his starts and stops; it was not, to say the least, a smooth ride. He tempered his accelerations with a touch of the brake and each attempt to brake was mitigated by a touch of the gas. Talk about your stop-and-go driving.

I don't know if he still drives that way, but it gives you an idea as to how bad habits can not only be developed over years of driving, but they can also be learned—or, I suppose in my buddy's case, taught. If no one's ever called you on it, you may not even realize that what you've been doing for years is actually a bad habit that could lead to a collision or a citation—or both. People get lazy until those bad habits one day give the driver a wake-up call. Try to get some training before that happens, because that wake-up call for you could mean death or injury for someone else.

☑ **Blue Light Bulletin:** Driving past the point where our skills have deteriorated will put us at risk for getting a ticket rather than a warning.

In those states like Washington—where the officer can request that the state retest demonstrably poor drivers to determine whether or not they should be allowed to keep their driver's licenses—you would be cited rather than warned in order for the state to have empirical evidence of your declining driving skills. None of us consciously wants to put our fellow citizens at risk because we no longer have the skills to drive safely.

Parking your car, for good:

How can we determine when this time comes? One of the best ways is to listen to our friends and loved ones when they begin to express concerns about our driving. A few years ago I responded to a call from the daughter of elderly parents, both of whom, in her opinion, were no longer able to drive safely. She had managed to convince her father to stop driving, but her mother held firm. Her mom's pride and independence impressed me, but her inability to see her own mental deficiencies saddened me. I was also downhearted because I could easily imagine myself in the same situation someday. I think a lot of us could imagine it. My empathy went equally to the mother and to her daughter.

I explained that although I sympathized with her, I had no authority to take her mom's license from her, prevent her from driving, or request she be retested by the Department of Licensing (DOL) without having seen her commit an infraction while driving. I told the daughter that absent a power-of-attorney, she could only use her influence as a loved one to persuade her mother to stop driving. The daughter asked me if I could at least talk to her mother from a police officer's perspective. I told her I'd give it a shot.

A fascinating woman, her mom was now in the later years of a long and wonderful life. She'd been a screenwriter and told me stories of her interactions with movie stars during Hollywood's heyday. I liked her very much and resisted what I was about to try, but I knew that her family, not to mention other drivers on the road, would appreciate it.

I first got her to agree that her friends and family were commenting more frequently about her driving. However, she still disagreed with her daughter that she shouldn't drive. I managed to convince her to contact the DOL and voluntarily arrange to be retested for her driver's license. I told her if she passed the test she'd have proof of her driving competency according to the state. I told her if she really thought her driving skills were up to par, she shouldn't be afraid to be retested. She agreed.

I left their house feeling I'd accomplished something, but also a bit melancholy at a possible glimpse into a crystal ball. The mom was content, certain she'd pass. Her daughter was satisfied, certain her mom would fail. I don't know what happened— whether or not she passed the test, or even if she'd taken it—but I haven't stopped her or responded to an accident involving her, so I'll just assume the best.

Ironically, a few months later an elderly woman (not the woman in the above story) struck and killed an elderly man while he was crossing the street only a few blocks away from where I'd had my conversation with the retired screenwriter. I don't know what kind of second-guessing the elderly woman driver, her family, or her friends will do, but I suspect there will indeed be some. At my age I can only imagine how difficult the decision to hang up the car keys can be. It's more than just a car that's being mothballed; it's part of a person's identity and independence.

Sometimes there's a strange calm that comes over more mature drivers. I once responded to a call at a local drugstore. An elderly man had attempted to park his car directly in front of the store's automatic doors when the vehicle suddenly lurched forward and struck them. Either his foot had slipped from the brake or he mistook the accelerator *for* the brake.

One of the reasons I remember the story so well is that the car struck the doors with sufficient force that it bent the metal frame, but it didn't shatter the glass. In fact, I couldn't find a single crack. But that's not the most remarkable part of the incident.

The store manager had met me outside; he'd been investigating the damage for himself. Apparently, after the incident, the driver had calmly backed up into the space where he'd initially intended to park. I asked the manager if the driver was all right. He said he must be because after the crash, he went into the store and just began shopping as if nothing at all had happened.

I went in and found him, half expecting to find an Alzheimer's patient. To the contrary, the man was tall and handsome, with dazzling white hair, a friendly smile, and bright, intelligent eyes.

"Hello, sir. You had a problem with your car earlier?"

"Well, my car had a problem with the front door to the store; I'm trying to stay out of it," he said with a smile.

I smiled back. "So, what happened?"

"I know what you're thinking: old man confused brake with gas, right?"

"Don't think old or young matters, but is that what happened?"

"Nope. No confusion; just was parking, turned to glance at an escaped shopping cart that was rolling free toward the back of my car. The way I twisted around, my foot slipped off the brake and onto the gas—then pow!"

"Well, that makes sense. Why didn't you wait for me to arrive?"

"At my age I only have so much time left; I can't waste it waiting around. Nothing I could do about it, right? So, I thought I'd get my shopping done. No telling how long it was gonna take you to get here. No offense." Again, he smiled.

"Oh, don't worry about that; with our short-staffing, I understand the sentiment. You have your insurance information for the store manager?"

"Yep, no problem."

●
●
●

This driver was in his late eighties, but his problem on this particular day was not age. He was sharp and articulate, and he appeared to be vigorous and strong. The thing that stood out for me was his attitude. He wasn't jaded or threatened because of his age; he was calm and confident because of his age. Never mind no ticket; I didn't even write a report, since the drugstore manager agreed to accept the man's insurance information and handle it civilly.

> ☑ **Blue Light Bulletin:** Giving up driving can seem like surrendering to age and time; it's hard to accept that this might be inevitable.

However, for some folks it just may be unavoidable. Perhaps it's best to prepare ourselves while we're still relatively young by making a deal with our future selves to watch for signs as we become older drivers—benchmarks that signal we might have to think about curtailing our driving, or give up our cars altogether.

Three serious things to think about:

1. Pay attention to things like getting stopped by the police more frequently when you've rarely, if ever, been stopped in the past.

2. Listen to comments about your driving from the people you love and trust.

3. And perhaps most important: Are you noticing some problems with your own driving? Will you have the courage to put other people's safety above the loss of some of your independence? If you don't face it, wouldn't it be a shame to have lived such a productive and honorable life only to end it—or worse, end someone else's—in a pile of twisted metal on some damp roadway?

Now, let's get back to getting you that warning. While most encounters will be between officers and motorists who differ in age to at least some degree, on occasion a traffic stop brings together those whose years on this Earth contrast significantly. You have the elderly driver who's been driving for six or more decades who gets stopped by the twenty-one-year-old rookie officer. If the elderly driver is a bit jaded, this is the time to put his ego in check. The fact he's been driving for half a century compared to the officer's five or so years doesn't change the fact that he's committed a violation.

> ☑ **Blue Light Bulletin:** If you expect the young officer to respect your age and experience, then you must return the respect—don't call him "Sonny" or tell him that you've been driving since before he was born, or even before his parents were born.

The officer may be young, but he's chosen a profession in which he serves the public, including you, at the risk of his own life and safety. Take the age out of the equation. If you blew it and pushed the red light, just deal with it honestly. Most officers, even the young rookie whippersnappers, are eager to respect your age and experience; don't give them a reason not to.

YOUR ORAL WARNING:

"Please don't look shocked that I approach your door with my hand on my gun. I am not getting ready to shoot you; I am just trying to keep it from making the same scratches down the side of your nice, new car that it makes down the side of my patrol car!"

—Sergeant G. Mason, U.S. Army MP

CHAPTER 12

Honesty Is the Best Policy

"Just relax . . . So how fast did you say you were going?"

In this chapter . . .

- ☑ How *not* to incriminate yourself
- ☑ Life will be easier when you admit you're wrong
- ☑ Cops are experts at detecting lies

You're just going to have to trust me on this one: Any good lawyer would advise you to remain silent after you're accused of a crime if the police want to ask you questions. This especially goes if you committed the crime. However, be forewarned: Having given you sound advice and fair warning, if I arrest you for a crime, it's my job to trip you up and get you to incriminate yourself.

> ☑ **Blue Light Bulletin:** It's hard to incriminate yourself if you're not guilty.

However, traffic infractions are a different matter. In most states the traffic code has been converted from criminal violations to civil infractions. The difference: You can go to jail for criminal violations, while you can only be fined for civil infractions. Even where traffic codes are still criminal violations, it's rare for anyone to go to jail for a minor traffic offense. It seems like a better proposition for everyone, although I suppose there are some folks who'd rather spend a couple nights in jail than cough up the money to pay their fines.

Examples of criminal violations:

Driving with Suspended License
Hit and Run
Negligent Driving
Driving Under the Influence (DUI)
Reckless Driving

Examples of civil infractions:

Moving violations:
Speeding
Failure to Stop for a Red Light
Failure to Stop for a Stop Sign
Failure to Yield Right-of-Way
Driver Inattention
Non-moving violations:
Expired Vehicle Registration
Expired Driver's License
Defective Taillight
Open Container of Alcohol

My point is, you'd be amazed at how most cops will appreciate a violator who admits what he did wrong, and further, apologizes—along with promising to try and never do it again.

"Oh, Officer," she says, before he's even gotten up to her window. "I can't believe I did that boneheaded move. I don't usually drive like that."

"Well, I was wondering why the heck you'd do that," the officer replied.

"The traffic lights are at an angle and I thought that one was mine—oh my gosh—I can't believe I—stupid, stupid, stupid," she says as she smacks her forehead with an open palm.

"Well, ma'am, we all make mista—" the officer begins.

"Oh no, Officer, I could have killed someone—I feel like an idiot—you should give me a ticket; I deserve it." She stops thumping her hand on her head and instead begins tapping her head against the steering wheel.

"Ma'am, I sure do appreciate your honesty, and you know what, I'm only going to warn you today," the officer says with a smile.

"That's so nice of you, Officer. I know I don't deserve it, but thank you."

"Okay, ma'am. You drive safely now." The officer waves as the woman pulls away from the curb.

"Oh I will, Officer, you can count on that," she says as she waves her hand out the window.

The woman keeps her smile locked on the cop in her rearview mirror until her car disappears around the bend. Once out of view, she begins to laugh out loud to herself. "Ha ha, sucker!" she snickers, kicking up her speed as she sees the signal light up ahead turning yellow.

The woman above thinks she's fooled the officer, and maybe she did, but officers are constantly aware that folks might be trying to get one over on them. When a cop encounters a person who seems honest, it's refreshing. Cops want to believe people are telling the truth for a change, that they're sincerely contrite. Besides, if they were lying, the only thing they got away with was not getting a ticket—I mean, no one died—and if she keeps driving like that, she'll eventually get that ticket, or worse.

Cops are lied to so often, they become experts at discerning the truth, the odd Academy Award–winning performance, such as the one above, notwithstanding. Officers are armed with highly advanced lie detectors, known in cop vernacular as *bullshit meters*, and known in the common vernacular as *ears*. When I contact a suspect or a suspicious person, I assume he's lying, and proceed from there. I do this because as good as I am at detecting a lie, people are sometimes equally as good at lying. The way I figure it, if their hearts are beating, they're breathing, and they're talking, then there's a good chance that they're lying.

When I contact the average law-abiding motorist, it's a real treat to speak with an honest person. When I hear, "Oh, I'm sorry, Officer; I don't know what I was thinking. I normally don't do things like that. I guess I was going a bit too fast. I should know better." Never mind not issuing the violator a citation—I want to issue a coupon for a free latte at the corner Starbucks.

I mentioned earlier that I once wrote a magazine article on this subject, geared toward motorcyclists, for *American Iron Magazine*. While conducting research for the article, I asked more officers about this particular chapter's title question than any other. The answers were universal: The truth usually helps, and even if it doesn't, it certainly can't hurt. If the officer is predisposed to write you up, then nothing you say will matter anyway.

> ☑ **Blue Light Bulletin:** Telling the truth is no guarantee you'll get out of a ticket, but if you get caught up in a lie or strangle yourself with a bad excuse, you're sunk for sure.

In that article, two police officers—one, a veteran traffic officer, the other a veteran patrol officer—provide a glimpse of the average officer's perspective on honesty during a traffic stop.

Traffic officer Wade Murray says, "Just being polite and adult enough to admit to getting caught goes a long way with me."

Patrol officer Mark Wong advises, "People lie and disrespect us all the time; try to be different."

"I'm sorry, Officer. That was a dumb move on my part," Mr. Fastcar tells the officer. "I was driving way too fast when I clipped that old lady's walker over there. Man, I can't believe I missed her. Good thing she didn't try to hang onto that thing. I mean, you should've seen it fly!"

I think we can all agree that Felix Fastcar was impressively honest. However, the idiot broke the first rule of my secret formula: How dangerous was the violation? Oh yeah, he'll get a ticket; most likely a criminal violation for reckless driving. But at least he'll get it served up by the officer with a heaping portion of appreciation for his honesty; not that it'll do Felix much good right now, but it couldn't hurt if he gets stopped for a lesser violation by the same cop another day.

Should I ask the officer for a warning straight out?

Why not? It's one of those things that really can't hurt, but (and this is a *big* but) be careful how you ask. If the officer gets the impression that you make a habit of driving carelessly and then attempt to cajole the officer into a warning without sincerity or contrition, even if he might have given you a warning, he may now issue you that citation feeling that you tried to "play" him.

How you present the question will have a significant impact. For instance, if you list all the cops in your family or those whom you know, once again, the cop may feel that you're trying to manipulate him. Incidentally, most cops I know resent having their names dropped by friends and extended family when on a traffic stop. We really don't care if you're Officer Jones's fourth cousin on your mother's uncle's godfather's side of the family, or if you were Officer Smith's dance partner in kindergarten.

If you're sorry for what you've done and you sincerely promise to not do it again, then why not ask. The officer might initially be in ticket-writing mode, and your overture may make him rethink it and possibly give you a warning. I have no problem giving this advice. I feel that officers should take direct responsibility for the tickets they issue. As long as we still have discretion in this job, it is our choice as to whether we issue a citation.

I try to never say to a motorist, "You're being issued this citation . . ." Instead, I try to say, "I'm issuing you a citation for . . ." This way, *I'm* taking personal responsibility. If someone asks me point-blank for a warning, I may reconsider if it's a close call (or I may not). If it's not negotiable, I have no problem telling motorists why I won't issue them a warning, and why they are getting a ticket. If I expect you to take responsibility for what you do, I expect I should take responsibility for what I do as well.

Stick up for yourself if you truly believe you didn't do anything wrong:

Now honesty doesn't mean admitting to a violation you believe you didn't commit. There are instances, although exceedingly rare (especially in my case), when police officers do make mistakes. Please keep in mind that a mistake is not the same as lying. The officer has his perception and you have yours. He may have missed something, but you may have as well.

In this instance I'm not saying you should apologize, but neither should you argue with the officer. After the stop, write down the facts as you remember them and choose to contest the citation. Present your facts in court, and who knows—the judge just might agree with you, or maybe at least reduce your fine. You might be surprised, but cops don't mind when you challenge a ticket. (Besides, it's good overtime for us.)

Honesty goes both ways, and despite what police critics would have you believe, honesty is important to most police officers. It doesn't take much to taint an officer's reputation, and his reputation is worth a lot to him.

Let me give you a couple of examples from my own files. I was on the stand testifying in a trial when the defense attorney gave me a copy of the incident report I'd written for the case. He pointed out that in one part of the report I'd indicated one time of day, while in another I'd indicated a different time of day for the same occurrence. I could have tried to cover it up with some excuse, but instead I answered that I'd made a mistake. I said it appeared I'd written the correct time originally, but then used correction fluid and replaced it with the wrong time.

When the defense attorney asked me why the discrepancy, I told him I didn't have a clue. The case was a couple of years old as it was, and I just didn't remember. What's the big deal? I'll tell you.

Maintaining integrity and building reputations:

I'd testified before this judge in the past and had built a reputation for honesty. When the defense attorney continued to badger me and tried to turn a municipal case into a federal one, the prosecutor objected and the judge sustained the objection and admonished the defense attorney to move past the issue. He said he believed it had simply been an honest error.

I remember my instructors teaching me in the police academy, my field training officer teaching me in the field, and admired fellow officers showing me over the course of my career, that lying just isn't worth the trade-off to avoid a little embarrassment, or to say what I think the prosecutor wants to hear. If my testimony helps the defense, so be it; it's justice we're after, not just convictions.

> ☑ **Blue Light Bulletin:** If an officer's honesty is important to him, so is yours. So be honest—you'll feel a lot better about yourself and you may even get off with that warning you're after.

Unfortunately there are those rare officers for whom your honesty means little. There's nothing I can do about that, but at least I can show you how you might keep your ticket count down to one rather than two, three, or more.

YOUR ORAL WARNING:

"My pet peeve: people who refuse to pull over and hope you will go away if they ignore you. When stopped they always tell you they thought you were after someone else because they didn't commit the infraction. Next in line are the folks who try to justify their actions, saying, 'Everyone does it. . . . Don't you have anything better to do than to harass honest, tax-paying citizens?' "

—Officer E. Lukaszeski, Seattle Police Department,
Traffic Unit, Motors

CHAPTER 13

Petty Tyrants

Dealing with tyrant cops: A sticky situation.

In this chapter . . .

☑ Definition of a petty tyrant

☑ Why some cops are petty tyrants

☑ How to keep petty tyrants happy

You've just placed your groceries in the trunk. You hop in the driver's seat, fire up your car, and head for the exit. As you turn out of the lot you realize you forgot something. You reach up over your shoulder, grab the seat belt, and strap yourself in. Ah, now you're on your way home to barbecue for a hungry family awaiting your mouth-watering summer fare.

Whoop! Whoop! A siren's chirp alerts you to flashing red-and-blue lights in your rearview mirror. Being a good citizen and a responsible motorist, you pull to the side to allow the patrol car to pass you to head to its emergency call, but it doesn't pass you; instead, the patrol car slips in and stops behind your car. Your heart's thumping; you're wondering what the heck you could have done. You hadn't even had the chance to accelerate past fifteen miles per hour yet.

The officer approaches. "Good afternoon, ma'am. The reason I stopped you is you failed to wear your seat belt."

"But Officer, I *am* wearing my seat belt."

"Don't try to pull that with me, ma'am. You are now, but you weren't a minute ago, were you?"

"You mean in the parking lot?"

"You didn't buckle up until you were actually driving out of the lot."

"Oh, you've got to be kidding me?"

"No, ma'am, I don't kid about the law."

"Can't you give me a warning?"

"No, ma'am, I'm sorry—I can't do that. Zero tolerance. Maybe if you had gotten your seat belt on while you were still in the lot, but . . . You know, I was rooting for you too."

I didn't make up this encounter; it reflects three similar incidents as related to me by three individuals, about three separate traffic stops in three different jurisdictions. One involved my daughter's friend; the other episodes involved two citizens who'd approached me in a coffee shop on two separate occasions within the same week—the week Washington State's new primary seat-belt law had just gone into effect. Previously, the seat-belt law was a secondary law; you could only be cited for failure to buckle up if you'd been stopped for a separate violation. With the adoption of the primary law, police officers can now stop a motorist exclusively for not wearing a seat belt.

Who, or what, is a petty tyrant?

> **Petty Tyrant:** The cop who, while not actually corrupt, serves as a de facto tax collector for his jurisdiction. He has poor judgment, little reasoning ability, and exercises no discretion. He thinks nothing of restricting a motorist's liberty for the least breach of the traffic code. No violation is too small to escape his notice. This cop not only aggravates commuters on their way to and from work, but he also annoys the good officers who try to carry out their mission and use their discretion in a reasonable fashion.

You might think it strange for a cop to refer to some of his comrades-in-arms in such a critical way, but when you think about it, who would know better? These bullies affect me as much (maybe more) than the motorists they stop. And, as you'll see in a future chapter, I fell into the clutches of a petty tyrant myself, so I'll admit it's also personal. But, in case you're wondering, I'm over it. No, really, I am. (Grumble, grumble, grumble . . .)

Law enforcement officers enforcing the basic traffic code have been responsible for capturing numerous criminals ranging from minor misdemeanants to violent felons. In fact, two of our nation's most infamous criminals, Oklahoma City bomber Timothy McVeigh and serial killer Ted Bundy, were both captured by officers enforcing traffic laws.

Regardless of the tangential benefits, some folks have a bad attitude about the police conducting traffic stops, because they think that petty tyrants abound. Some folks think *all* cops are petty tyrants. I was listening to a radio program several years ago discussing police behavior, and how cops no longer enjoyed the benefit of the doubt from the public, the media, and the courts as they once had. One caller made this jagged comment: "I think every person who becomes a cop has to be at least a little bit fascist."

I was blown away by this comment—not because I wasn't used to antipolice rhetoric in a liberal city, but because the comment was delivered so matter-of-factly by what seemed to be an otherwise normal, intelligent woman. She didn't even seem to have any animosity in her voice when she made her observation.

I have to admit that her words stung me. Some might be thinking, *The truth hurts, huh?* Well, those of you thinking that can just stop that nonsense right now. I think that the comment stung me not because it's some dark secret I keep hidden within me, but because I'm one of the most libertarian people I know. When I show up at a meeting and someone says, "Please, take a seat," I respond, "Don't tell me what to do." (Okay, old libertarian joke, but it still tickles my funny bone.) In fact, most street cops I know lean toward the conservative and libertarian end of the political spectrum. Cops, street cops in particular, are generally staunch, unapologetic defenders of our Constitution and of citizens' rights.

Most cops are content to let you go about the business of conducting your life in a peaceful manner, until you breach that peace and inhibit someone else's right to do the same. It's the petty tyrant who is out looking and waiting for you to screw up. To him it's an "I gotcha" game, and he doesn't care that he's the only one who knows that you're both playing.

The truth is, you rarely meet the officers who conduct their patrol shifts in a reasonable manner, those who only stop people who are putting others at risk, because they're not the officers who are snatching your liberty for frivolous violations. The reasonable officer sees a minor infraction, but chooses not to stop you, because he's determined it was inadvertent and put no person or property at risk. He observes no additional errors and you appear to be a safe motorist. See, you got another warning and you never even knew it.

The officer who'll pull you over for three over the limit or for rolling slowly through a stop sign at a deserted, unobstructed intersection with a clear three-mile view in all directions at 8:00 A.M. on a Sunday morning, and tickets you even though you took responsibility, apologized, and have a spotless driving record, gives all officers a bad name with the general motoring public.

It's natural to remember the negative encounters with the police over the positive ones:

You might get four warnings from officers over many years of driving, but you're going to remember the one officer who stopped you as you were going about your daily routine, just to write you for three miles over the limit or for a seat-belt or a helmet violation—believe me; I know.

It doesn't take many of these petty tyrants to give all officers a bad name with the public. An overly aggressive ticket-writing officer can affect hundreds of people a month, people who tell other people about the stop. Stopping people is nothing but a revenue or stat-raising game to petty tyrants. Each month is a chance to get more tickets than the last month, to ingratiate him- or herself with the hierarchy by filling their jurisdiction's coffers. This officer doesn't see the law-abiding motorist as a person trying to go about his daily life as a productive community member; he sees him as a yummy statistic. He's not as interested in motorist safety as he is in using deceptive means to catch violators, such as setting up a virtual ambush of people putting on their seat belts as they leave a grocery-store parking lot.

However, I really can't go on without mentioning another facet of this type of officer which can't be ignored. It doesn't forgive the petty tyranny, but it may mitigate it no matter how much we wish it didn't. The other thing about the petty tyrant, which is strange, but true, is if you're involved in a wreck on the freeway, there's a burglar in your house, or you're being assaulted by some dirtbag on the street, he's going to rush to your assistance. He'll risk his life to pull you from a burning car, arrest the burglar who's broken into your house, or risk his safety fighting off your attacker. Remember, to him the law is the law. He'll do his job to the letter, whether that means writing you a chippie traffic ticket or saving your life. So even *he* deserves your (albeit reluctant) benefit of the doubt.

> ☑ **Blue Light Bulletin:** If a petty tyrant stops you, be respectful anyway. Not because you like how he does this portion of his job, but to be practical, because he's the kind of cop who might give you several tickets. Being civil and polite just might keep the ticket count down to one.

YOUR ORAL WARNING:

"Keep your hands visible and stay in the car unless told otherwise. Try to remember that the officer doesn't know you. He doesn't know if you have a weapon in the car, or if you might be fleeing from a crime that has yet to be reported. Try not to be rude. No one I've stopped has talked me out of giving them a ticket, but plenty of people have talked me into giving them one."

—Detective K. Kizzier, Seattle Police Department,
Sexual Assault & Child Abuse Unit

CHAPTER 14

Alive Is a Good Thing to Be

"Now there's a good sign he'll get off with a warning . . ."

In this chapter . . .

☑ Officer safety is a top priority

☑ Determining threat levels

☑ Officers are held to impossible standards

Officer safety is always uppermost in rookie officer Donnybrook's inexperienced but tactical mind. He's aware of his entire surroundings at all times. No one's going to do him in; at least not without getting his own belly full of hot lead. (Sorry, couldn't resist the *Dragnet* lingo again.)

Officer Donnybrook is out patrolling his district when he pulls Aunt Mabel over for rolling through a stop sign. Never mind that there isn't another car in sight or sound, and he can see Aunt Mabel is somewhere between ninety-eight and one hundred and two years old. That doesn't matter to Officer Donnybrook; the law is the law, and Aunt Mabel has just broken it.

Donnybrook practices good officer-safety procedures as usual, and broadcasts his stop over the radio so other units are aware of his location. He exits his vehicle, dons his cap, adjusts his sunglasses, and cautiously approaches Aunt Mabel's faded green '69 Volvo.

Donnybrook checks the trunk; it's locked. You never know—Aunt Mabel might be a cleverly disguised criminal hiding an accomplice in the trunk. The backseat also checks clear.

"Good afternoon, ma'am. I'm Officer Donnybrook. Do you know why I stopped you?" he asks, his eight-point hat's shiny black brim so close to the top edge of his sunglasses he has to tilt his head backward to see. He palms his gun nervously.

"Oh, I'm sure I don't, dear; why don't you be a good boy and tell me," Aunt Mabel says as she begins digging around in her handbag, which more closely resembles a piece of luggage.

"Ma'am, please keep your hands where I can see them." Jimmy unsnaps his holster and rolls the strap forward.

"Well, I'm sure you want to see my license, now, don't you, dear?" She continues digging in her purse.

Jimmy steadies his bladed stance. "Yes—but, I haven't asked you for . . . Ma'am, please take your hands out of that bag—I have to see your hands—Ma'am, your hands—let me see your hands *now*!" Jimmy steps back, firms up his shooting platform, and locks his hand around his holstered service weapon's Pachmayr grips.

"Oh, don't get yourself all in a dither, young man—oh, wait a minute; I know where my license is," Aunt Mabel says as she finally withdraws her hands from her bag. Jimmy sighs and relaxes a bit. Then, all of a sudden, Aunt Mabel lunges across the front seat and flips open the glove compartment.

The rookie snatches up his weapon and draws down on Aunt Mabel in one deft motion. "All right, ma'am," his voice squeaks and cracks. "That's it—get out of the car right now and—"

Okay—the above story might be ever-so-slightly exaggerated, but it goes to illustrate a common thread that runs through everything cops do: officer safety.

Officers are taught that you can't help anyone if you don't get there in the first place, or if you get yourself hurt or killed needlessly. Officer safety education often involves officers recounting anecdotes, which illustrate useful lessons to student officers pointing out other officers' mistakes and experiences. Many stories are about officers who've been injured or killed in the line of duty in an unexpected way, when least expecting it, by the last person from whom they'd expected it.

Expecting the unexpected:

I'd been a cop for less than a year when a seventy-five-year-old woman assaulted a fellow officer. Believe me, the minute a cop thinks he's seen it all, as I said in an earlier chapter, the universe brushes him back with a wicked slider to keep him on his toes. The point I've been meandering toward is this: When Officer Friendly, or even rookie officer Donnybrook, stops you for what you believe is a minor traffic offense, put yourself in the officer's glossy black shoes.

> ☑ **Blue Light Bulletin:** The cop doesn't know you. And you know, it's kind of weird if you think he should.

You may be 100 percent positive you mean the officer no harm, because you're in a unique position to know; the officer, however, is not. Until he has assessed the situation and has determined the threat level you present, he'll remain on edge to some degree.

Sometimes people mistake this caution for rudeness. Hell, some people even become offended that the officer would ever entertain the notion they could possibly be a threat to anyone; they must believe they possess a transparent mind and soul. Hey, until the cop has assessed you, he's not about to bet his life on the hope you're not Machine-Gun Kelly's great-great-grandniece about to revive an old family tradition.

Not long after I came on the job, a young detective was shot and killed. It was my first in-the-line-of-duty death since becoming a police officer. It was the first time I'd shrouded my badge with a traditional band of black, and the first time I attended a police funeral. Unfortunately, cops get hurt and killed every day in America, but it's not every day that it hits home.

While of course a tragedy, the detective having left behind a wife and children, the specifics of the incident made the event even more so. I mean, what's more egregious than harming someone who's simply offering you a helping hand?

It was early evening when the detective was rolling down a freeway ramp. He saw several people near an apparently broken-down vehicle. The detective stopped his car, parked, got out, and approached the group to see if he could lend his assistance. As he approached, someone in the group of (we know now) thugs recognized him as a police detective, pulled a gun, and opened fire.

The detective was able to draw his own weapon and return fire, but not before he'd been struck in the torso by one of the suspect's bullets. The detective made his way back to his car and managed to drive himself to a nearby police precinct. Officers attended to him while he provided information on his murderer. Fire department medics arrived and quickly transported him to a downtown trauma center. In the end, the damage was too extensive. The young detective—the good Samaritan, who'd simply stopped to try to help stranded motorists in need—died of his wounds a short time after arriving at the hospital.

This is an example of what's in the back of every officer's mind when he approaches your car. It's not in yours—but maybe it should be. While the detective had been dressed in plain clothes, the suspect shot him because he recognized him as a police officer. It's not hard to realize that a patrol car and uniform would have been immediately recognizable, and it's likely that these same suspects would have opened fire on any police officer who'd stopped to investigate or offer assistance to this group.

Just imagine the evil in a person who would kill someone who'd stopped to help them. Does it make you squirm to even think that we share our planet with people like this? You may not be able to imagine it; perhaps you are able to block it out. For the police officer, it's a constant threat. For us, that wicked person could be sitting behind the wheel of the next car we stop.

On some occasions, while cops may not die, the system can almost make death seem like the easier alternative.

The call blared out over police radios all through the precinct: "Vehicle into a concrete bulkhead—at least four on board—fire responding."

"Two-Henry-oh-one, en route—I'm close," Officer Carlin responds.

On arrival Carlin observes the vehicle straddling the side-walk—its front end smashed into the concrete retaining wall. Inside the vehicle are one injured teenage boy and two young adult men who appear to be assisting the boy. The fire depart-ment EMTs and medics have just arrived on the scene.

"Okay, you two," Carlin points to the men still in the car. "Come on out and talk to me." Another officer had arrived, and other officers were approaching the scene from all directions.

"We're just trying to help," says the one called Lewis.

"That may be, but the medics are here to treat them; I need you to come here and talk to me," says Officer Carlin.

"Screw that. We don't need to talk to you," Clark, the other man, says as he starts to walk away.

"Hey, get back over here. *Stop!*" Carlin orders, and begins to walk toward Clark, who'd begun to trot away from the scene.

As Carlin steps in Clark's direction, Lewis darts toward Car-lin and punches and kicks the officer; Carlin's ballistic vest absorbs the blows. My partner and I arrive at this moment. Two other officers are now grappling with Clark. A large crowd has gathered, and it's only a matter of time before more will join in the fracas. The melee is full on. Sirens can be heard coming in from all over the city.

I start toward Officer Carlin's position when I observe a third suspect running toward Carlin, closed fist raised toward his blind side. I intercept this man who, upon seeing me, adopts a fighting stance. I reach out to grab him, but he runs away. Another officer eventually arrests him.

There is one part of the story I've held back—the 90 percent of the iceberg neither the men, nor the hostile crowd that had gathered, could see. It's a stolen car.

I resume my track toward Officer Carlin when I observe six agitated young men walking toward Officer Carlin. I approach them.

"They don't have to be doing that; they're just trying to help the kid out," the apparent leader says to me. He's a handsome kid with an athletic build and long braids in tight rows.

"That may be, but the officer is only trying to get him to cooperate," I say.

"Cooperate with what? They were just trying to help that kid," the same young man says.

"I understand, but that's a stolen car. We had information there were four people in it at the time of the crash, and some ran off, but they weren't sure about that," I explained. The looks on their faces tell me they'd gained an instant collective understanding of the situation. No one had considered the car might have been stolen; they realized that this bit of information changed everything.

When Officer Carlin had arrived at the smashed car, he had information that a stolen car had crashed with four suspects on board, some of whom may have fled. Carlin observed three people in the car. Until he could determine otherwise, they were all considered possible suspects. The officer didn't even attempt to handcuff the men as he could have—and perhaps, should have; instead, he merely ordered them to come to talk to him so he could investigate their part in the incident. He needed to find out whether they were good Samaritans, suspects in an auto theft, or perhaps even witnesses to the fleeing suspects. Fire department medics were now tending to the injured kid, so their first aid was no longer necessary.

Had the men simply come over to speak with Officer Carlin, no incident or arrests would have occurred. However, the men chose another path: to obstruct an investigation and to assault police officers.

A municipal court jury acquitted the defendants. Did the jurors believe the suspects were innocent of the charges? No. Adding insult to insult, after being polled, the jury consensus was since the suspects had been physically restrained and one had been pepper-sprayed during his arrest, *the poor men had suffered enough.* Don't think that ridiculous and convoluted verdicts like this, which fail to follow the law or common sense, don't have consequences on police officers and the way they perform their jobs, even traffic enforcement—they do.

Never good enough:

Verdicts like these color how an officer views the average citizen. People too often view the police with suspicion and contempt. They fail to give officers the benefit of the doubt they need in order to do their job. Police officers are held to an impossibly high standard. If a situation goes sideways and the officer is pressed to use force, some see it as the officer's failure and not the criminal's. Some people refuse to acknowledge that you just can't reason with some people. They continue to disparage the officer until one day, they find themselves on the receiving end of a criminal's dark heart.

A simple misunderstanding:

While cops have to keep officer safety uppermost in their minds, drivers need to understand this so they can keep their own safety highest in their own minds. One of the reasons I wrote this book was to convey the misunderstandings that can often arise when two parties come together in a critical moment, and one of the parties doesn't understand what the other is up to. Once again, this is where the benefit of the doubt comes into play. When directed by the police, it's always best to comply fully, and if you have questions, they can be addressed later. In most circumstances the cops are more than happy to explain why you were treated in a particular manner, once the situation has calmed down.

And then there's being at the wrong place at the wrong time:

Jeff walked into the new Mexican fast-food restaurant and ordered a meal. He'd been meaning to try the place, and here was his chance. The restaurant was clean, the service friendly, and the aroma of cilantro and jalapeño made his mouth water.

Jeff collected his bag of food, bid the cashier *adios*, returned to his pickup truck in the parking lot, and began to hungrily consume his dinner. He only lived about a mile away, but the food smelled too damn good to wait. He switched on the stereo and enjoyed some tunes while eating.

Ten minutes later he crumpled up the bag and tossed it onto the passenger floorboard. He started up his truck and headed out of the lot. He hadn't gotten two blocks before he heard a siren chirp and looked to see flashing lights in his rearview mirror. He reached up over his shoulder and quickly fastened his seat belt as he pulled into the parking lot of a closed business.

Jeff waited for the officer to approach, kicking himself for forgetting to put his seat belt on. *What a stupid thing to get a ticket for*, he thought. But rather than seeing an officer approaching his car, he heard a voice come over the loudspeaker. He looked back and saw two marked (and one unmarked) police cars, all with lights flashing and twirling.

"Driver—shut off the engine."

Jeff turned the key and the engine died.

"Driver—place the keys on the roof of your car."

Jeff rolled down his window and tossed the keys on his truck's cab.

"Driver—open the driver's door and slowly exit the vehicle; do not turn around."

Jeff got out and turned to face the source of the voice. He squinted into the blinding spotlights aimed at him.

"Driver—I told you not to turn around; now, turn around."

Jeff stood confused for a moment; was he supposed to turn around now, or was he not supposed to turn around earlier, or what?

"Driver—face away from me," the officer clarified.

Jeff turned around, happy to get his eyes out of the bright lights.

"Driver—walk backward toward the sound of my voice until I tell you to stop."

Jeff began to walk slowly backward.

"Driver—stop. Now, get down on the ground on your belly, spread your arms and legs out from your sides, and turn your head to the right."

Jeff had no idea that the cops around here took their seat-belt law so seriously. He decided right here and now he'd never again forget to buckle up. Immediately following this thought, he felt the pressure of a strong man's knee on his back. His hand was wrenched behind his back as handcuffs clicked shut around his wrists. The officer leaned him one way and then the other way, frisking him for weapons. Jeff was pulled to his feet and leaned up against the car.

"Just stand right here for a minute and we'll explain what's going on. Look over there toward that patrol car coming into the lot."

Jeff faced the car, the spotlight came on, and his eyes squinted shut.

"It's a negative," came the broadcast over the loudspeaker.

"Negative; it's not him. Uncuff him," a sergeant said.

An officer took a handcuff key out of his shirt pocket and removed the cuffs from Jeff's wrists as the sergeant began explaining what had happened.

"What's your name, son?"

"Jeff," he answered as he rubbed his wrists. "What'd I do?" He didn't think confessing to the seat-belt thing would be helpful at this moment.

"Well, as it turns out, nothing. Were you at that new Mexican place down the street?"

"Yeah, got some dinner, ate in the lot, and then I was headed home. That's when you guys stopped me."

"Okay, that makes a little more sense now."

"Maybe to you," Jeff said.

"Well, while you were in the lot eating, someone went in and robbed the place at gunpoint."

"You gotta be kiddin' me! Really?"

"Really," the sergeant assured him.

"So, why'd you pull me over? I didn't rob them."

"We know that now, but here's the description they gave us when they called 911: white male, six foot, one hundred and eighty pounds. What're you?"

"Six-one, one seventy-five," Jeff answered.

The cop nodded. "And he left eastbound driving a red, mid-sized pickup. Whatcha got here, Jeff?"

Jeff smiled and shook his head. "You've got to be kidding me . . ." he said, staring at his red Dodge Dakota pickup truck.

"Nope. While you were eating in the parking lot, a guy matching your description pulled into the other side of the lot, robbed the place, and took off in a truck like yours. You pulled out and took off in the direction of the robber just as our first unit arrived. He saw you, called it in, and the rest, as they say, is history."

"No way," Jeff said, scratching his head.

"You have any questions, son?" The sergeant asked. "You understand why we did what we did?"

"Hell yeah; now I do."

"By the way, you did really well following the instructions; you've never done that before, have you?" the sergeant teased.

"No way; not me," Jeff said.

"Well, good job, Jeff," the sergeant teased him again.

"Yeah, thanks—I guess. You won't be offended if I'd rather not meet you guys like this again?" Jeff smiled.

"Actually, we'd prefer you didn't, Jeff. You take care. Hope the rest of your night is less eventful."

"Yeah, me too," Jeff said as he started up his truck, buckled up, and drove off.

> ☑ **Blue Light Bulletin:** Understand that getting stopped because you or your vehicle matches a description can conceivably happen to anyone; it's even happened to cops.

This story illustrates something that could turn into a serious misunderstanding, even in someone who's innocent getting shot. Any one of us could be on the other side of that loudspeaker in similar circumstances. In general, these situations are rare, although in certain high-crime areas, they can occur with greater frequency.

You're going to be confused if something like this ever happens to you. Having read this account, hopefully you can tuck it away somewhere and it'll come back to you in the unlikely event that you ever get stopped as a result of matching a suspect's description.

And sometimes we cops act no better than the ordinary citizen, allowing our emotions to override our common sense. Every law-abiding person, including cops, would like to think that their goodness and innocence is so apparent, no one could possibly mistake them for a criminal. Well, I'm here to tell you, and remind others, that criminals come in all shapes and sizes, and some of them are shaped just like you and me.

The best thing to do in this situation, and I'd argue, the *only thing* to do, is simply comply with the demands of the officers. The more you delay or hesitate with following instructions, the more likely it is that you'll make the officer's guilty-meter rise. Be embarrassed, indignant, whatever, but most of all, be cooperative. That way it'll be over quicker and you can get back to your life with a story to tell, or at least something to grouse about to your family and friends.

You think the police should be fair and equitable, right? Off-duty police officers should be as liable for minor traffic infractions as any other citizen, correct? This is a tricky subject, but hang around a bit and I'll show you why one officer letting another officer off with a warning rather than writing him a ticket is a good thing—for you.

YOUR ORAL WARNING:

"If you want us to know something, tell us before pen goes to paper."

—Officer E. Lukaszeski, Traffic Unit, Motors

CHAPTER 15

Please Press Hard, Officer–Four Copies

Car-ma.

In this chapter . . .

☑ Officers write other officers tickets

☑ The importance of discretion

☑ If a cop won't stand up against a bad law, who will?

This is another tricky subject. I say tricky because there are some people who believe law enforcement should be blindfolded like Lady Justice, and all statutes should be equally enforced to the letter of the law. For them this includes officers writing traffic citations to other officers for minor traffic infractions.

I shouldn't have to, but let me make a quick disclaimer: I'm talking exclusively about *minor* traffic infractions here, not major traffic or other non-traffic crimes. If an officer causes other cops to have to arrest him because he dishonored his uniform and his fellow officers by intentionally committing a crime, then I hope that officer gets what he deserves.

This means within the law and department policy, he'll enforce the law according to his discretion. Discretion is important, as no two incidents are exactly alike. The officer is the one on the scene at the time, and is in a much better position to decide what should be done according to the specific circumstances of the moment—not some stuffed shirt behind a desk that hasn't tromped a beat in a decade or two.

The officer who uses his discretion properly and exercises it fairly understands how to deal reasonably with law-abiding, hardworking motorists. Many officers will approach the average stop inclined to issue a warning to the motorist, unless the motorist employs the techniques I've enumerated to change the officer's mind.

All I can tell you is, if you're truly interested in getting that warning, then I ask you, who would you prefer stop you—the officer who would write his fellow officer a ticket for rolling through a stop sign, or the officer who uses his discretion and doesn't write the officer a ticket due to professional courtesy, not to mention common sense?

I say common sense because it's not out of the realm of possibility that two officers could find themselves working together someday. Here in Washington State, the 1999 World Trade Organization riots in Seattle brought together officers from agencies all over the state. How would you like to be standing in a riot line, one of twenty-five officers facing an intersection crowded with 10,000 protestors, positioned right next to a state trooper you wrote a ticket to for five over the limit in his personal vehicle last Saturday? Yeah, not good.

And as long as we're on the subject—one that brings back traumatic memories for me—let me tell you a story about a cop writing another cop—me—a ticket.

Even ticket masters get tickets, too:

Once upon a time I was riding my motorcycle back to Seattle from Wenatchee, Washington, on a beautiful Sunday morning. I had just spent a wonderful weekend riding with some fellow Iron Pigs (the Iron Pigs Motorcycle Club is an international police/ firefighter Harley-Davidson club). We'd gone over to support our brothers and sisters at the Yakima Police Department's annual motorcycle show and fund-raiser, Show and Shine.

We were riding up a grade into the scenic Cascade Mountains when a state trooper passed us in the opposite direction. Of course, being cops, we all silently acknowledged a brother on the job on such a gorgeous Sunday morning.

My instant affinity for him was premature, as he'd made a sudden U-turn and I saw his blue flashing lights behind us. We pulled our bikes over to allow him to pass to go to an emergency call. Instead, he pulled in behind the last rider.

You see, this state has a helmet law. The trooper wrote me a citation for violating that law, despite the fact I *was* wearing a helmet when he stopped me. In fact, I was wearing a helmet that had the labeling and other ridiculous items the law allegedly required at that time, and despite the trooper never physically inspecting my helmet, he'd somehow *divined* it was in violation and cited me. He didn't cite me despite my being a cop; I believe he cited me specifically *because* I was a cop. He said I should have known better.

That he didn't approve of cops riding Harleys who were clad in black leather was obvious. One of my buddies, a retired twenty-nine-year police veteran, asked the trooper, "Do you write a lot of cops?"

With a sneer the trooper answered, "I write a lot of *these*." He pointed to my helmet.

I won't bore you with the facts I discovered (you can thank my wife for that), but I studied the law and found it was flawed in its construction and enforcement. I decided to challenge the citation. Instead of launching into my "There's a special place in Hell for cops who write other cops" diatribe, I'll get to the bottom line. After a trial, during which the burden of proof had been mine—I still have the court transcripts and tapes to prove it—the judge found me guilty.

After I proved my helmet complied in every way with the law as it was written, the judge ruled (yes, with a straight face) that my helmet was illegal regardless, because (you're gonna love this) the labeling had partially worn off. She compared the worn labels on a helmet with the worn tread on a tire and with a defective headlight—implying, I guess, that if the labeling wears off a helmet's internal or external portions, even if only partially (and as with mine) worn off the interior fabric, the helmet must be tossed into the trash. I searched several thesauri, including my favorite, *The Highly Selective Thesaurus for the Extraordinarily Literate,* by Eugene Ehrlich, for an appropriate synonym for the word "ridiculous" that could do justice to the judge's ruling. I had no luck. (Again, I'm not bitter.)

Cops know how you feel after you get a ticket:

I'd be lying if I didn't admit the trooper stopping and citing me affected me on an emotional level. Although I have little respect for that particular trooper, and frankly think that there *is* a special place in Hell for cops like him, I have a great deal of respect for the Washington State Patrol. It is among the best state patrol agencies in the nation—they are among the best traffic-collision investigators in the world—and as with any government agency they have some bad apples within their ranks. Some apples are a little wormier than others.

The experience definitely made me more empathetic with the average motorist stopped for a traffic violation. Aside from the personal issues, this stop affected me to the point where I had to do something more effective than whine to my wife and anyone else who would listen.

I contacted a woman who was active in the local motorcycle-rights community. She's a remarkable woman and an effective lobbyist. After discussing the resolution to my helmet ticket, she asked me if I'd be interested in testifying before the Washington State Legislature's Transportation Committee—against the motorcycle helmet law. I was hesitant at first, but then thought: *If a cop won't stand up against a bad law, who will?*

I testified in favor of a repeal of the state's mandatory helmet law. I should clarify my position: I support a motorcyclist's right to choose whether or not to wear a helmet and a motorist's right to buckle up or not. I always wear a seat belt when driving my personal car; I made that adult decision long ago. I also always made sure my children were latched in. However, I'm adamant in my belief that the government has no business telling adults how to protect their own bodies while engaged in a legal activity.

Bottom line—if you want a warning, then you want a cop who gives other cops warnings. You want a certain ticket, then you want a cop who will write his fellow cops tickets.

Just a thought:

When you see a cop who's got someone pulled over, do you ever think to yourself: *Why doesn't that cop just leave him alone*? Have you ever been pulled over and you've insulted the cop by asking if he has anything better to do, not having the faintest clue as to what call he investigated just before he stopped you? If so (or even if not), read on, because you never know.

YOUR ORAL WARNING:

"If you are issued a citation, remember it is just that—a citation. It happens to us all at one time or another, and if that's the worst thing to happen in your life, then you're doing pretty darn well. On top of that, sometimes we all need a reminder to pay more attention to our driving habits. Being in the traffic unit and seeing the results of way too many accidents has really driven that point home to me."

—Officer E. Lukaszeski, Seattle Police Department,
Traffic Unit, Motors

CHAPTER 16

You Never Know

Even after lending a hand, being a cop can leave an officer tired and deflated.

In this chapter . . .

☑ Things are not always as they appear

☑ Assumptions during traffic violations

☑ Crisis, trauma, stress, back to work

I'm going to divert in this chapter from the lighthearted to the serious in order to make an important point. As you've seen, a police officer's job is not lacking in humorous events, but it's not always a laugh a minute either. There is a saying that police work involves long hours of boredom interrupted by moments of stark terror; I can attest to this. To be better able to put yourself in the cop's shoes, which will better position you to get a warning, you have to try to understand the extremes his job sometimes requires.

Let's delve into this a bit . . .

The next few stories are not about traffic stops, which is intentional. I need to use them to illustrate some of the calls the officer may have investigated just *before* he stopped you. Another story shows you that when you see another poor slob stopped by the cops, things are not always as they appear.

Too many people make erroneous assumptions about the officer. I once helped a couple from Maryland change their flat tire at a tight intersection in the Arboretum. The nice woman said something poignant to me. "I suppose people don't come out of the woodwork with video cameras when you're changing people's tires, now do they?"

"True, but don't worry," I said. "Someone might see me with this tire iron and think I'm about to beat you with it; then they'll stop and whip out their cameras."

I loved that woman. *She gets it.* I almost wished something else was wrong with her car so I could help her some more.

You've driven past an officer who appears to have someone stopped for a traffic violation. We all have. Do you think: Ha, he got one! (And it's not me.) Or are you like some others who think: That's all cops do all day, harass people. If you're in the latter category, let's see if the following story doesn't make you reconsider.

"Holy crap! You see that?" my partner asked me, pointing to the car ahead of our patrol car.

"Oh man, that thing looks like it's about to fall off," I said as I activated my overheads and chirped the siren. We pulled in behind the vehicle.

"Good afternoon. I stopped you because it looks like your left rear wheel is about to fall off," I told the teenage boy.

"You're kidding, Officer! I hit a curb kind of hard coming out of a parking lot, but I didn't think it did any damage."

"You couldn't feel your car wobbling?"

"Nope. Not a bit."

"You have a spare?"

"I think so." The kid popped his trunk latch and got out of his car. He opened up the trunk. "Looks like just one of those small doughnut-looking things," he said.

"That'll have to do. Just don't drive on the freeway with it and change it as soon as you can," I told him.

"I've never changed a tire before; could you help me?"

Pathetic, I thought. What are they teaching kids these days, when a kid can't even handle a simple tire change. *Geez.*

"Yeah, we'll give you a hand," my partner said. He repositioned our car to better block traffic and I began to rummage through the kid's trunk, looking for the jack and tire irons, when a voice popped off from the sidewalk.

"Hey, they can't do that!" The voice belonged to a lean man in his fifties, his thinning hair pulled back into a gray ponytail.

The kid looked around and realized the man was talking to him. "Do what?" the kid asked.

"Check your trunk; they need a warrant to do that," the man said with authority.

"Excuse me, sir, this really isn't any of your busi—" I began to say.

"I'm not talking to you," the man said, as if speaking to me left a bitter taste in his mouth.

"I'm just looking out for you; they do—they need a warrant," the man repeated. The kid remained silent, confused at his would-be hero's attempt to rescue him.

"So, we need a warrant to do this, eh?" I asked the man.

"You're damn right you do—and you know it," he said.

"You hear that?" I said to my partner as I pulled the car jack from the trunk. "We need a warrant to help this kid change his tire."

"Wow," my partner recoiled in mock disbelief. "I really should keep up on those Supreme Court rulings."

I wish I were a good enough writer to adequately describe the look on that man's face when he realized we had stopped the kid to help him change his defective tire and not to harass him, but I'm not sure even Walt Whitman could have done justice to the man's expression. The man toddled off toward his house. I followed him for a few steps trying to get him to tell me what it was that made him assume the worst about the police. He mumbled something as he disappeared into his house about cops kicking his friend's door down years ago.

You never know.

☑ **Blue Light Bulletin:** Assumptions often come into play, not only when you see someone else stopped, but when an officer stops you for a traffic violation.

Oh, brother:

You have no idea what call the cop has just handled before he stopped you for speeding. Your first comments could be more damaging toward your goal of a warning than you know. I'd ask you to try putting yourself into the officer's place. The patrol officer or deputy sheriff might have just come from the homicide office or the sexual assault unit after conducting a preliminary murder or rape investigation just before he saw your infraction and stopped you. The incident may have even involved a child. The state trooper may have just wrapped up a fatality collision investigation in which multiple people were killed just before he stopped you while on his way back to the barracks.

I doubt many people think about this aspect of an officer's job: crisis, trauma, stress, and then back to work. Perhaps people are too conditioned to television cop shows, where one event is handled per episode and then the officers get to go home after solving the case. You've heard the admonishment: Never assume. Here's why . . .

"Officer, please don't kill him," the stocky man said nervously as he smoked his cigarette out on the porch. The man was referring to his brother, who was still inside the house. The call had come in as a domestic violence assault involving two adult brothers, one off his medication for mental problems.

"Is he still inside?" Officer Daniel Rand asked.

"Yes. I think I broke his arm; I had to hit him with a dumbbell bar—I threw it in that room right there," the brother said, pointing to the first room on the left.

"Is he armed?" Rand asked.

"Yeah, that's why I came out here—he has a big knife."

"Okay, you stay out here." The officer, along with two backup units, cautiously entered the house. Once in the living room, the suspect made his presence known. The big man stood in the kitchen growling, his wild, wiry, gray-black hair spilling down into a similarly savage beard. He was wearing a plaid flannel shirt and blue jeans. Only the bottom half of a Dutch door separated the large man from the officers. Above his head in his left hand he held a large butcher's knife.

"Stay back or I'll kill you," the man said in a raspy voice.

"Police—drop the knife!" Officer Rand yelled as he drew his weapon with his right hand and his pepper spray with his left.

"I don't care who the hell you are, I'll kill you all," the man said. Blood had soaked through the right sleeve of his flannel shirt.

"Drop the knife or I'm going to pepper-spray you," Officer Rand warned.

"No—I'll kill you!"

The officer raised his pepper spray and applied a burst into the man's face, emptying close to half the propellant. The oily spray had some limited effect, but the suspect continued to menace the officers with the knife. His eyes were now almost closed—tightened to small slits. The officers noticed the door to the backyard was open. They decided to try to make their way around back to prevent his escape.

Officer Rand remained in the living room, covering the suspect. The Dutch door and the suspect's obscured vision remained the only barriers keeping the armed wild man away from the cop. The other officers had gone around to the back of the house to get another angle on the suspect—and to prevent his escape. Officer Rand repeatedly yelled at the suspect to drop the knife.

"I can't see you, but I can still kill you," the suspect yelled, stepping toward the Dutch door.

Officer Rand knew he had to make a decision. He determined the point at which he'd use lethal force. If the suspect made contact with the Dutch door, even though he was already three times closer than his training had dictated was prudent, he'd have to fire.

The suspect began to move forward. The officer raised up his .38 revolver aimed at the suspect—center mass—moved his index finger inside the trigger guard, and prepared to fire. He placed pressure against the trigger, a shot imminent, when the suspect finally lowered the knife and backed further into the kitchen. Remarkably, it didn't appear the officer's actions had motivated the suspect, as his eyes appeared to have remained tightly shut. His beard was drenched in pepper spray and slimed with thick snot running from his nose.

The other officers made it to the rear of the house, diverted the man's attention, and sprayed the suspect again, whereupon he dropped his knife. Weapons holstered, all three officers grabbed the suspect. Officer Rand grabbed the suspect's right arm, which made a gruesome crunching sound and bent in a direction the arm wasn't meant to go. Rand could see a bone protruding from the suspect's skin because he could see it moving within the bloody fabric of the man's sleeve. Unable to handcuff the suspect, the officers brought him outside to better restrain him. As the officers escorted the man down the old wooden steps, one of them observed that the man had another knife.

"Knife!" the officer yelled as he pushed the man forward. Rand and the third officer also pushed away from the man, causing him to topple down the steps and onto the patio like Saddam's statue crashing down in the center of Baghdad. "On his wrist—another knife; it's tied to his wrist with rubber bands," he pointed out.

We managed to handcuff the man and recover that knife, as well as four more knives he'd hidden on himself. In all, officers had recovered six knives from the man. After medics stabilized his wounds, they transported him to the hospital.

The backup officers soon cleared the call and went back to duty, but before logging into service they stopped for a cup of coffee and a casual debrief. They sat down in the café to enjoy their well-deserved break.

They'd been in the shop for five minutes when a professional-looking woman strolled into the store. She slowed to a saunter as she passed the officers' table and with a sneer remarked, "Our tax dollars at work, eh?"

You never know.

> ☑ **Blue Light Bulletin:** Remember that whenever you see an officer, you have no idea as to the nature of the officer's previous call. Following any call I can think of—other than an officer being significantly injured or involved in a shooting—the officer will more than likely return to the streets after completing his portion of the investigation.

Consider this next story and try to imagine going back to your regular job afterward.

A ten-year-old boy, fear frozen on his face, his black bangs hanging in his reddened eyes, met officers out on the damp sidewalk.

"My mom—she's dead. He killed my mom!" he managed to blurt out, ibetween sobs. He pointed up the steps to a second-floor apartment. His mother was up there, and a man had knocked him out of the way and was hurting her. His dad was still at work. The officers immediately asked the boy to show them where his mother was, but the boy cowered near the fence gate. "No! I'm afraid—I can't go up there. You go help her."

The officers ran up to the apartment to find the suspect standing in the living room, next to the Christmas tree, flipping through the victim's checkbook. A bloody knife sat on the kitchen counter next to the sink. The victim was lying on her bedroom floor, bleeding from an obvious stab wound to her abdomen. The officers quickly took the suspect into custody as one officer secured him, while the other began first aid on the gravely wounded victim. Shortly after, other officers arrived on the scene and took control of the suspect.

The two original officers watched helplessly as the light of life left the young mother's eyes and she expelled her last breath with an eerie hiss. They performed CPR until the fire department arrived and took over care of the woman. They later found out the suspect had stabbed her once in the stomach, but five or six times in her back.

Once the scene was under control and the victim was on her way to the trauma unit at Harborview (the hospital where her husband worked), the officers put the story together. The family had provided the suspect with a place to stay for a few weeks. Although he had recently moved out, he'd returned to the apartment angry, pounding on the door. The victim called the police. Her ten-year-old son stood trying to block the door, but the suspect kicked the door in, knocking the boy to the ground.

The suspect entered yelling at the woman about some money he claimed she owed him. He grabbed a kitchen knife from a drawer and stabbed the woman in the stomach. She screamed and turned to run but he caught her and stabbed her repeatedly in the back. She somehow managed to get to the phone in her bedroom and called 911. At first she was screaming into the phone, but soon her cries diminished to shallow, raspy breathing. At that time, a dispatcher broadcast that she'd managed to get the woman to calm down, when in fact, the woman was dying. Her son had been hiding behind the Christmas tree watching the suspect viciously murder his mother before his ten-year-old eyes.

The homicide detectives arrived and took over the investigation. After the officers completed their written statements, they returned to duty. They hoped they wouldn't get any more calls for the remainder of their shift. However, one officer was forced to make a stop when a motorist ran a red light and nearly caused a collision. He pulled the man over and walked up to the driver's window.

"Good evening, sir. Do you know why I stopped you?"

"Nothing better to do tonight?" the motorist replies.

You never know.

The stories in this book are based on actual events in which I took part, or they have been recounted to me by trusted fellow officers. And while some stories were tweaked for editorial and entertainment purposes, nothing has been altered to change the essence of the incidents. In the case above, the story is true to the last detail. I know; I was the officer who, along with a fellow officer, performed CPR on the dying young mother. She was pronounced dead later that night.

> ☑ **Blue Light Bulletin:** Things officers are required to perform daily are things that most people will never do in a lifetime.

The next time you see an officer relaxing in a coffee shop, try to remember that an hour ago, he may have been performing CPR on a stab victim, or someone who had been thrown through the windshield of a car. Again, you really just never know.

A ORAL WARNING:

"If you are going to backtalk the officer and request the supervisor . . . don't have warrants [out for your arrest]."
—Officer H. Crossland, Lancaster Police Department,
Texas Traffic Division

CHAPTER 17

I Am So a Cop–Really!

"But dude, you're only a bike cop."
"The key word is 'cop,' kid."

In this chapter . . .

☑ A matter of respect
☑ An officer is an officer
☑ Pull over when you see blue lights!

Cops come in all shapes, sizes, and varieties, as diverse as the general public. However, I want to focus on differences other than physical, psychological, and political—I want to focus on different types of cops with regard to specific unit assignments, some of whom might surprise you as they pull you over. Officers work a variety of beats.

> **Beat:** The geographic area regularly covered by a police officer while conducting his duties. This could be as small as one busy block in a business district, a neighborhood, or even a place like rural Alaska—vast expanses requiring air or sea travel to traverse.

Some work in patrol cars while others are on foot, bike, horseback, motorcycle, boat, helicopter, airplane, Jet Ski, snowmobile, or with a dog. For some reason, certain assignments may bring the officer less respect from the public than others.

Police, forms of transportation, and levels of respect:

Cops in cars get about as much respect as a police officer can expect in that at least people recognize them as traditional law enforcement officials. What can you say about the mounted patrol? Everyone loves horses. Who needs respect when people actually like you? Motorcycle cops probably get more respect even than cops in cars; sitting atop their gleaming Harley-Davidsons, BMWs, or Kawasakis and sporting dark sunglasses, black leather jackets, and boots, they cast an ominous shadow. Other cops may disparage motor cops. Some say motor cops rarely exercise discretion, appear unfriendly, and are rumored to be so hard-core they'd even write themselves a ticket if they caught themselves violating a traffic law. But not me; I'd never ridicule one of my two-wheeled brethren. But we'll talk more about that later.

There have been occasions when I've observed an ordinary motorist give a police officer short shrift simply because that officer didn't conform to their idea of what a cop should be. For example, bicycle officers get respect from pedestrians and from other bicyclists, but sometimes not from some motorists. Consider what this officer experienced with a violator who worked above and beyond the call of duty to get himself a ticket.

The beautiful, candy-apple-red BMW sat at a stop sign waiting to proceed northbound across the intersection, about to disregard a right-turn-only sign mounted below the stop sign. Officer Mike Kerfuffle had seen this type of behavior before. Perhaps the motorist simply hadn't noticed the sign.

Mike rode up to the driver's side window and informed the thirtyish male motorist of the right-turn-only sign mounted on the pole below the stop sign. The motorist looked Mike up and down. Mike was in full bicycle-police uniform, complete with a black helmet bearing the word POLICE in large white letters. The motorist looked back at traffic, ignoring Mike's repeated attempts to dissuade him from committing this dangerous traffic infraction.

Traffic cleared and the red Beemer shot through the intersection. Mike took off after the speeding car. He broadcast over his radio that he had a motorist who was failing to stop for him. The motorist finally stopped. While he could have easily outrun Mike, perhaps he suddenly became aware that patrol cars may not have been far off, and he'd decided he couldn't outrun Mike's radio.

Mike approached the violator's window, which was rolled down. Before Mike got a word out the violator said, "What's your *problem*?" He emphasized the final word.

Now we've talked about this before, haven't we? Is this any way to begin a conversation with someone who has the authority to diminish your net worth?

"My problem is, you ignored my instructions to obey the traffic sign on the other side of the intersection and you failed to stop for me when I directed you to. I need your license, registration, and proof of insurance."

"I don't have those things with me."

"Where are they?"

"I forgot them at home."

"Is this your car?"

"Yes. It's mine."

"Okay," Mike said, pulling out his notepad. "Give me your name, address, and phone number."

The young man provided the requested information and said, "Are you going to write me a ticket?"

"No, sir, I'm going to write you several tickets."

"Then I'm going to call my lawyer. I've beaten every single ticket I've ever gotten."

"Suit yourself," Mike said with a shrug.

In the meantime, Curtis arrived in his patrol car to stand by with Mike in case any problems arose. Mike ran the man for outstanding tickets and any wants or warrants issued using the patrol car's computer. The Department of Licensing database was returning information slowly; Mike decided not to wait, and issued the tickets based on the information he already had. If the guy was wanted, some other cop was gonna have to grab him up.

Mike returned to the BMW driver's window and presented the ticket for his signature. As he held it out he explained the man's options in handling the citation.

"Do you have any questions, sir?" Mike asked as he practically shoved the ticket book into the driver's hand. The man refused to take the pen or the book.

"I'm not signing that," he said. After all of the problems he'd already given the officer, he capped it off with a refusal to sign. Mike explained that the driver wasn't admitting to any guilt, and by not signing he could end up going to jail for the weekend. He still refused to sign.

Mike decided to give Mr. Beemer one more chance. He pulled out his crystal ball and gave the man a glimpse into his future. "Sir, here's what's going to happen if you continue to refuse to sign: I'm going to call a sergeant out to the scene. If, after the sarge explains to you what I've already told you and you still don't sign, I'll be slapping these shiny bracelets onto your wrists and you'll be off to the gray-bar motel for a day or two."

The man sat quietly for a moment, then lowered his head, resigned to his fate. He finally took the pen and signed the ticket. Mike asked if he had any questions; the man said no and drove off. He didn't drive far, as he pulled up about ten feet and parked illegally, blocking a driveway to an apartment building. He may have been resigned to signing the ticket, but his ego still had one last gasp. He got out of his car, walked behind Curtis's patrol car, and with exaggerated movements, as if he were a stage actor, he wrote down the license plate number.

Curtis looked at Mike and said, "That's gonna help." Mike grinned. Both cops followed the man with their eyes as he walked to the front of Mike's bike and recorded the police bicycle's number. Curtis looked back at Mike. "Now that's really gonna help," Curtis said. Mike's grin grew wider. Both cops shook their heads in awe at the display of passive defiance as the man returned to his car and drove off, bringing an end to the drama. Mike thanked Curtis for the backup and they each rolled on back to their patrols.

Why in the world do people behave like Mr. BMW? Nothing he did was to his advantage, and if we rewind to the initial contact, all he had to do was make the flipping right turn at the right-turn-only sign, and none of what followed would have happened.

It's truly amazing. I once stopped a guy for going straight across an intersection despite a right-turn-only sign. When I stopped him, he told me the sign was confusing and he hadn't known what to do.

"Sir, you just had to turn right," I explained.

"But the sign said right only. I knew I couldn't go left, but it didn't say I couldn't go straight," he said.

"Sir, it should be sufficient for the sign to read right turn, but not only does it read right turn, it also has an arrow indicating that traffic should turn right, so you get pictures too. And in addition to right turn, the traffic engineers have kindly added the word, *only*, a very restrictive word indeed. I don't mean to be snotty, sir, but it sure seems like the city went out of its way to make that sign clear. Am I making sense?" I said, as I allowed myself a shallow sigh.

"Well, it still doesn't make any sense—maybe there should be a light," he said.

Education wasn't working at all with this driver. I reinforced the lesson with a ticket. Perhaps that would give him more reason to reflect, or at least to turn right at the next right-turn-only sign he sees.

Here's a quick one for you. Above, I showed you what can happen if you fail to give the proper respect to a police officer riding a bicycle. Now let me tell you about an experience I had with my Field Training Officer (FTO). It may cause you to continue to obey all the traffic laws, even when it's just the paddy wagon behind you.

My FTO and I had been assigned as Unit 2, Sam 10 one day. Sam 10 is the prisoner van for the South Precinct. The dark-blue Chevy Astro van was outfitted with police insignias, emergency lights, and a siren. We were driving southbound on I-5, returning from dropping off a vanload of trustees to their facility in the north end. We were cruising in the far right lane at the speed limit. Other motorists were also at the speed limit, indicating a proper respect for a police vehicle in the vicinity, when a group of young men in a small brown car pulled in behind our van and began tailgating.

My FTO, one gruff man, was in no mood to play chicken with a carload of punks, but he also wasn't in the mood to make a traffic stop either—avoiding work being preferable to actual work. He moved the van into the next lane in order to allow the little brats to pass. Instead, they moved into our lane and resumed tailgating. My FTO was unusually patient that day; once again he moved back into the other lane to disengage the carload of teens who were laughing at their own stupidity.

Once we'd moved, the kid driving, instead of tailgating, stayed in that lane and raced forward and began pacing us in the adjacent lane. His passengers had become emboldened and were flipping us off and yelling out the window. My FTO was the model of patience; he looked straight ahead and tried to ignore them so they'd go away. I have to admit, I was disappointed in him at that moment. He'd always seemed like a man of action in this type of situation. I'd later learn that the last thing he wanted was to get into something while doing prisoner-van duty. "Sarge says to do transports, not police work," he told me later.

Tired of their game, the driver suddenly pulled ahead at a high rate of speed and immediately swerved over, cutting off a few cars and nearly causing what could easily have been a horrendous collision. I looked at my FTO; I could tell what I'd just seen was an idiot straw breaking a pissed-off camel's back. My FTO cranked the pedal to the floor and the van lurched forward. He switched on the overhead red-and-blue lights and popped the siren on to a constant wail. We caught up to the carload of heathens in short order. With screaming siren and flashing lights behind the car, I could see the occupants were no longer laughing or flipping us off. The faces I saw were dead serious.

They began to slow and eventually came to a stop on the freeway shoulder. I asked my FTO if he wanted me to get out and write them the ticket. He told me no; he said I was too new, and didn't know enough violations to write them for, so he'd better do it himself. I asked him if I should come up to the car with him— he said, "No, you'd better not." He wasn't smiling.

I'm not sure how many tickets he wrote them. I didn't ask.

> ☑ **Blue Light Bulletin:** When you're driving down the road and you see anything with wheels—or with hooves, for that matter—and if it has any lights, stickers, or placards indicating the vehicle or animal is law enforcement, you'd best err on the side of caution and give the officers the respect they deserve, as well as a wide berth.

YOUR ORAL WARNING:

"I like the old joke about the trooper who stops a guy for rolling a stop sign. The guy tells the trooper, 'Well, I slowed down for it. That counts.' The trooper replies, 'If you don't understand the difference between slow and stop, I can demonstrate it with my nightstick. . . . If I were hitting you with it, would you like me to slow down or stop?'"

—Cpl. J. Davis, Avondale, Arizona, Police

CHAPTER 18

Electra Glide in View

" . . .You're kidding me, right?"

In this chapter . . .

☑ Motorcycle cops' primary mission

☑ Motorcycle cop stereotypes

☑ Advantages for them, disadvantages for you

Being too tough on oneself:

"Damn!" veteran motorcycle officer John Skulls growled as he reached for his radio.

"Tom forty-one—traffic stop."

"Go ahead, Tom forty-one," the four-pack-a-day voice answers.

"I'll be at Tenth and East Union."

"Do you have a plate for me, Tom forty-one?" the dispatcher asks.

"Well, uh—radio, the thing is—I've stopped myself." John

clicks the microphone off, leans his bike onto its kickstand, and grabs his ticket book.

Silence.

"Tom forty-one? Did I copy you correctly? You're making a traffic stop on yourself?"

"That's right, radio: I ran a stop sign at Tenth Avenue and East Union Street—just missed the darn thing."

"Umm, received. I've got a traffic control call waiting; should I hold it for you, or dispatch another unit?"

"Negative—hold it for me, I won't be long. Oh, and I'm under control."

"Okay. Um—copy—" The dispatcher's coarse voice stretches the word *copy* out incredulously.

Officer Skulls leans against his leather saddle and shakes his helmeted head. "Stupid, stupid, stupid . . ." he repeats as he smacks his helmet with a leather-gloved hand.

This is definitely an over-the-top "fictional" glimpse into the daily life of a motorcycle officer—a police officer who's normally been in the department for a number of years and, once highly trained to operate a police motorcycle, is assigned to a department's traffic unit, or in smaller departments, as its sole traffic unit.

☑ **Blue Light Bulletin:** The motor officer's primary mission is to enforce traffic laws, provide traffic control, investigate traffic incidents, and conduct dignitary escorts, among other duties that may arise.

The motorcycle cop is often viewed (sometimes even by fellow cops) as the mysterious rider wearing dark sunglasses and clad in black knee-high boots and black leather jacket who would, even if he's Catholic, write the Pope a speeding ticket. Okay, perhaps I'm exaggerating—a tad—but old stereotypes die hard. Regardless of this perception, these officers fulfill an important function in law enforcement, because sometimes some people drive so badly, they kill. The simple truth is, knowing there may be a motorcycle cop lurking around the next corner keeps people from driving worse than they already do. (Ain't *that* a scary thought?)

Once I was driving to the old police headquarters downtown on a rainy day. I was about to turn into the parking garage when a motor cop pulled up next to me. With a sneer on his face he said, "You'd better get some mud flaps on that thing." He then rode off without a hint of civility. After parking my *thing*, a brand-new Jeep Wrangler, I checked to see if my tires extended past my fenders. The dealer had installed extended fenders to cover the wide tires, but to be honest, I have to admit that upon closer inspection the tires did extend possibly 1/16th of an inch out from the fenders. Either that motor cop was having a bad day, or he's got the eyes of an eagle—probably both.

The thing that got me about this interaction with the motor cop was the lack of basic civility. How does this behavior foster better relations between motorists and police? It doesn't. It also doesn't do any favors for the next cop down the road who meets up with the guy who's been the recipient of a cop's unwarranted rudeness. Now, while I feel cops shouldn't necessarily treat people as if they're customers at Nordstrom's or Macy's, we should initially treat the average driver with at least a basic level of respect. However, there are those motorists who purchase an immediate lack of respect through their manner of driving, the lousy condition of their vehicle, and their attitude. I'm not saying it's right, but cops are human, and these things have an effect on us. In my case, I was driving a brand-new vehicle, I was driving safely, and I even cast the officer the most un-cheesy and sincere grin I could muster; after all, he was a brother cop—right? There was no reason for him to be so gruff with me, but like I mentioned earlier, I don't know what call he'd just handled before our little interaction. A fatality crash, perhaps—possibly involving a child? At any rate, he certainly deserves the benefit of the doubt—we owe him that much.

Cops on motorcycles have it tough:

I'll concede motor cops have a difficult job and, being a daily motorcycle commuter myself, I know they deal with more idiot drivers than those of us on foot or in cars. A motorcycle is a great way to get around (and in my opinion, it's the way of the gods), but there are a few inherent risks one should be aware of.

Too many drivers fail to pay enough attention to what's going on around them, and they refuse to grant the same courtesy to the two-wheeled rider that they might give a four-wheeled (or eighteen-wheeled) motorist. Still, as a vehicle the motorcycle has many advantages, but that's something you'll have to discover for yourself one day, if you're fortunate enough to have the Harley bug bite you.

A motorcycle on a mission:

While the motorcycle cop's authority is identical to the patrol cop's, their primary missions are different. The motor cop's primary mission is to focus on traffic enforcement. In many jurisdictions, such as in Seattle, they aren't tied down to 911 calls, although they can and do respond to assist patrol officers if they're in the vicinity of a high-priority call. Conversely, patrol officers often swing past a motor officer's stop to make sure they're okay.

It is the motor officer who most strikes the fear of Zeus into motorists. Like hungry cheetahs waiting for the plump gazelle to zip past, cops on motorcycles can conceal their locations more easily than a patrol car; they can maneuver swiftly through heavy traffic; and being assigned to the patrol division, they're more likely than the average patrol officer to issue you a ticket rather than a warning. This is not a criticism; it's their job to focus on traffic enforcement.

I'm not saying you'll never get a warning from a motorcycle officer—I know many who give out warnings all the time—but they still give out a lot of tickets too, specifically because, again, that's their job. The odds are against you once you've been stopped, however, because motor cops are out in the thick of it all day, and they tend to stop the more flagrant violators. As a patrol officer I see lots of stupid things motorists do, but I don't have the time to get to most of them. Motor officers don't have the time to get every violator, but they do have time for more than I do while on patrol.

> ☑ **Blue Light Bulletin:** One of the main aspects of a motor officer's job is to watch for people who make mistakes on the road and then teach those motorists a lesson.

I paint a gloomy picture, don't I? You're probably wondering if you have any chance at all of getting off with a warning if a motorcycle cop stops you. Well, of course you do; but let's say if your chances with a patrol officer are 50/50, maybe better, maybe worse, with a motor cop you're looking at more like 30/70—sometimes maybe better; sometimes maybe worse. The same rules apply as with any other officer during any other stop, maybe more.

The motor officer has a tough job. Not only does he have to deal with the worst that motorists have to offer, but much of his time is taken up with traffic control. I defy anyone to maintain their civility (and sanity) after doing traffic control for just five minutes. Seriously, go ahead and try it!

As a patrol officer I do traffic control occasionally, but not nearly as frequently as the motor officer. Of course, I see my fair share of crazy drivers while controlling traffic as well. I swear some folks think people crash just to ruin *their* day.

I was once directing traffic in the Washington Park Arboretum. A nine foot, six inch U-Haul rental truck had lost a battle with a nine foot, one inch stone Roman arch bridge, peeling open the container like a sardine can, spilling furniture out for a hundred yards. I took a position at the north side of the bridge and another officer directed traffic to the south. We coordinated our efforts so that traffic could pass in alternate increments of about a minute each. A minute's worth of southbound traffic would flow, and then a minute's worth of northbound traffic.

The collision had occurred at dusk and it was getting progressively darker. I armed myself with my trusty flashlight and mounted on it what a colleague of mine humorously refers to as a hunter-orange prophylactic. At any rate, it's an orange cone attachment for the end of a flashlight to make the officer more visible at night. As cars approached, I'd repeatedly raise and lower the flashlight, blowing my whistle until I was convinced that the motorist had seen me and had indeed stopped to wait for oncoming traffic.

Once certain the cars had stopped, I radioed to my counterpart that he could allow northbound traffic to flow. With no reason to watch the traffic I'd stopped, I kept my attention focused on the approaching traffic to make sure it flowed smoothly and didn't run over yours truly. The other officer radioed to me that he'd stopped traffic flow, and after the last car passed me, I could open up my end. After the last car passed I turned and took a step toward what I thought would be the gap between me and the waiting southbound traffic, and immediately fell onto the hood of the—supposedly—waiting car.

While I was busy staying alive, monitoring oncoming traffic, one stealth-mode driver had, unbeknownst to me, crept up, inching his way until he was literally centimeters from my leg. Now, I agree with you if you feel that I should have been paying more attention, for officer's safety sake, but what can I say? *My bad*, I blew it. I have to admit it, though—I'd overestimated the common motorist's ability to follow directions and, oh yes, this too—to use common sense.

Now, if I have to endure this type of situation on an occasional basis, can you imagine if you had to deal with such things on a routine basis? Imagine you're a clerk at a fast-food restaurant. You've just taken the order from a customer. You tell him to wait there a moment and you'll be right back. You go into the back to place the order and when you turn around, guess who's blocking your path? You can transpose this incident to many jobs, but there's something about police work that brings out the *weirdest* (you thought I was going to say, *worst*—right?) in people. So, give the motorcycle cop a break.

R-E-S-P-E-C-T:

Surely Aretha can't be wrong; listen to her advice and treat the officer with respect. The motor officer, when it comes to traffic enforcement, is the model of efficiency. He'll slap paper on you faster than you can say *Electra Glide in Blue* because he's well-practiced at it. Therefore, if you're honest, accept responsibility, and he senses you are sincerely contrite when he speaks with you, that may cause the officer to pause for a moment, to put a comma in the stop rather than driving straight toward the period. Even if the officer doesn't give many warnings, you may be the lucky *one* for that day. At any rate, if you're not honest, respectful, and civil during your interaction with the officer, don't count on getting off with a warning.

With the abovementioned virtues in your quiver, you're properly armed if stopped, but you may never need them. You've turned over a new leaf, decided to drive better, and not give Officer Law any reason to pull you over. That's all fine and dandy, but while your driving may be approaching perfection, what's your rusty, rolling bucket of bolts up to? Let's move on and see how your car can get you into trouble even if you're driving along, just minding your own business.

YOUR ORAL WARNING:

"Back in the day, I stopped a female for excessive speed. Before I could say anything, she stuck a star in my face and said I couldn't write her a ticket because her [significant other] was a deputy sheriff. I told her, 'In that case, bring him to court so that I can apologize to him for the ticket I am going to give you now.' Never did get to meet him."

—Lt. J. Davis, Chagrin Falls Township Police Department (Ohio)

CHAPTER 19

That Jalopy of Yours

"I don't need to explain the reason why I pulled you over, do I?"

In this chapter...

☑ Be organized with your vehicle paperwork

☑ Don't give a cop a reason to pull you over

☑ Keep your vehicle in good working order

I'll never get over the number of people who shouldn't be driving—in fact, who probably shouldn't even be a passenger in a car—who seem to have no problem giving an officer a reason to stop them. There are people who shouldn't be driving because their license has expired, has been revoked, or has been suspended. There are other people who, while still authorized to drive, have outstanding warrants issued for their arrests. You'd think these people would drive like Aunt Mabel on her way to the casino on Sunday, but no. They speed, run stop signs and red lights, and have expired registrations or defective equipment on their cars. Instead of blending into the woodwork, they provide an officer with multiple reasons to stop them. Hell, they practically challenge the officer *not* to stop them. They may as well mount a taxi-like lamp on top of their car, displaying—instead of FOR HIRE—STOP ME.

> ☑ **Blue Light Bulletin:** Remember this admonition: Don't give the cop a reason to stop you. All the good driving in the world won't help you one bit if your car gives the officer a reason to stop you.

Keeping your vehicle in good working order will help prevent you from getting stopped in the first place. Also, keeping a well-maintained vehicle will be obvious if you are ever stopped, and may show the officer that your vehicle is mechanically sound and you just hadn't noticed yet that your right brake light is out. This is an easily forgivable offense. Follow my other rules, and he just may let you off with a warning.

Reasons you can get pulled over:

Expired registration tabs, improper license-plate display, burnt-out lights, broken lenses, dragging mufflers, wobbly wheels, unsecured loads, tire-tread wear, broken mirrors, improperly displayed license plates—just to name a few!

After I pull someone over, which sometimes includes an arrest, I usually ask the motorist why they'd give the police any reason at all to look at them twice. Almost everyone gives the standard seven-year-old kid's response: "I don't know." I give the ones that are at least smart enough to attempt to drive within the law some credit, but then to get stopped for a broken taillight is just plain dumb.

Look, I'm a cop, and I've got to ask—again—why give cops any reason to give your car a second look? Murphy's Law dictates you'll be driving along, obeying all the traffic laws, just minding your own business, when something will go terribly wrong. You'll be pulling out of a parking lot when a police car slips in behind you. You're not worried because you're driving carefully and haven't broken any laws. Still, those red-and-blue lights blast into your rearview mirror. *Uggh!*

You pull to the side of the road, wondering what you did wrong. The officer arrives at your window. "Good afternoon, ma'am. Do you know why I stopped you?"

You think later about what a dirty trick that question was, but right now your mind is a swirl of thoughts and you can't seem to catch one; you begin to babble.

"Was I speeding? Did I cut someone off? Did I fail to signal? I'm not sure, Officer," you spill forth. For future reference, the better answer to that question is "No." (And for any cops out there who flinch at my providing that advice, in the heat of the moment no one's going to remember that tip anyway, so get off my back.)

The officer smiles; it's nearly imperceptible, but it's there. "No, I didn't see you do any of those things. The reason I stopped you today is because you have a defective taillight."

"Oh, Officer, I've been meaning to get that fixed," you reply.

This is where honesty runs into quicksand.

"You were aware that your light is defective, ma'am?" the officer says, more scolding than inquisitive. The officer has to balance the fact that you've ignored a safety defect in your car with your honesty. After all, you could have lied to him and told him you didn't know your taillight was broken.

"Yes, Officer. I'm sorry; I'll get it fixed right away, I promise."

"Well, let me see your license, registration, and proof of insurance. I'm going to run a routine computer check. As long as you don't have any outstanding tickets, I'll go ahead and give you a warning this time. But if I see you driving again and you haven't fixed that light, I'll give you this ticket. Deal?"

"Deal. Thank you, Officer."

☑ **Blue Light Bulletin:** Remember: An officer may be inclined to let you off with a warning for that stop sign you rolled through, but he may still slap you with a broken-taillight ticket. Don't give him the choice.

The woman blasts through the stop sign; she knows she did it, and at that very second she sees a patrol car sitting on the corner, out of her peripheral vision. *Shoot!*

"Good afternoon, ma'am. Do you know why I stopped you?"

"Not really," she lies.

"Really?"

"What did I do, Officer?" she asks, innocent as all get-out.

"Ma'am, you failed to stop for the stop sign back at Twelfth and Aloha."

"Really? I thought I stopped, Officer."

"Ma'am, I can't believe that you're telling me that with a straight face. Can I see your driver's license and proof of insurance, please? Pull it out of the holder, please. Thanks."

"Oh, Officer, I'm sorry. Could you give me a warning?"

"Well, I may have considered that, but I can't very well give you a warning for something you say you didn't do, now can I?"

"What do you mean, Officer? You can give me a ticket or a warning, right?"

"Yes, but if I warn you, it's because you're sorry for what you've done wrong. You told me that you haven't done anything wrong, so what would I be warning you for?"

"For what you think I did."

"Sorry, ma'am, I don't pull people over for what I *think* they did; I stop people for what I *know* they've done."

"Oh, I know you're right, Officer. I'm sorry; sometimes I don't think very well when I'm nervous. I know I didn't stop. Tell you the truth, I saw it too late and didn't want to skid."

"Now that's some honesty that I can appreciate. Could you please sign here, ma'am?" I ask as I present the ticket book and pen.

"But, Officer, you're still going to write me a ticket? I said I was sorry."

"You did, but you sure made me work for it, didn't you?"

"Yeah, but couldn't you give me a break anyway?"

"Sure. I'm giving you a break. I'm not going to cite you for running the stop sign. However, I noticed that your left brake light is out, so I'm going to give you a ticket for that, which is an administrative equipment violation and not for the stop, which is a moving violation."

The woman signs the ticket. She's not exactly happy, but she knows it could have been worse.

The thing I'm trying to impress upon you in this chapter is that it could have been better, too. After the initial problem, the motorist had come to an understanding with the officer and it appeared that his efforts to educate her had been successful. Hell, he may have even let her off the hook completely—if she hadn't had something mechanically wrong with her car. This provides officers with an additional tool of enforcement; sort of a way to impress the lesson on the driver, short of issuing a moving-violation citation, which can negatively affect a driver's insurance rates. If the woman's car had been without a flaw, in this particular scenario, the officer would likely have let the woman off with an oral warning.

YOUR ORAL WARNING:

"Advice to family members, friends, and our rookie officers when they first get on: 1) Have your paperwork together and ready. 2) Keep your hands visible. 3) Be honest, admit your wrongdoing, and don't make whiny excuses."
—Craig Nelson, Deputy U.S. Marshal, former Army MP, Traffic Unit

CHAPTER 20

Born to Be Wild–or Mild

Expecting the unexpected.

In this chapter . . .

☑ Be predictable when you move

☑ Remove your helmet

☑ Keep your documents handy

Although individual motorcyclists are as varied as any other group, there are basically two types of riders. There are the motorcyclists who see their bikes merely as transportation, a museum piece, or sports equipment. Some of them might even commute by bike, but to those riders their bikes are no different than their cars; they're just easier and cheaper to park and they use less gas. Their motorcycles collect dust in the garage until the next warm sunny weekend arrives, when they can ride for a couple of hours to inflate their spirits. (And there's absolutely nothing wrong with that.)

Then there are the *bikers*. These are the motorcycle riders who have fifty-weight motor oil running through their veins. They eat, sleep, and breathe their motorcycles. They ride as often as possible, and their motorcycles are the most significant part of their lives next to their families (who run a very close second). I've even heard that some claim their bikes as dependents when filing their taxes, but I'm sure that's just a wild exaggeration.

Whether your bike is simply two wheels and an engine that you ride on occasion or when gas prices soar, or whether you carry a picture of your scooter in your wallet, have RIDE TO LIVE— LIVE TO RIDE tattooed on your forehead, and wear spark-plug ear-rings, there are some issues specific to all motorcycle riders that should be considered if you want to improve your chances of get-ting off with a warning.

As I mentioned earlier, I first expressed the idea for this book in an article I wrote for *American Iron Magazine*. Although the advice I provide in this book is of as much help to motorcyclists as it is to any other motorist, there are some special considera-tions to keep in mind when you're stopped by the police while riding a motorcycle.

For one thing, a motorcyclist is not physically enclosed within a compartment as is a car driver, which has both benefits and liabilities for the officer's safety. A motorcyclist's movements are more easily observed than a car driver's; however, the driver can more easily conceal a gun within the interior of an automo-bile in order to ambush the officer, while a motorcyclist is better able to physically attack the officer if he is so inclined, being able to move swiftly from the bike. Also consider that helmets, espe-cially the full-coverage style, conceal the motorcyclist's identity and also provide protection for the rider if he assaults the officer, causing the officer to use physical force to fight off the attack.

It's important to understand these aspects of a traffic stop from the officer's perspective if you want to make your interac-tion more amiable and the results more palatable. When you see the blue lights or hear the siren's chirp, you should pull to the right side of the road. Begin to pull over immediately, but don't cut over suddenly or dynamite your brakes; roll to a smooth stop. A five- to eight-hundred-pound motorcycle can maneuver and stop more quickly than over a ton of police car. You don't want to piss off the cop by stopping short and causing his coffee to spill all over his lap and ticket book, do you? Instead of that warning you're hoping for, all you'll get is a soggy citation.

Once you've pulled over, move predictably. By that I mean, don't jump off your bike and rush back toward the officer, but don't move like you're the subject of an NFL slow-motion replay either. Move normally. Shut down your engine and lean your bike onto its kickstand. Place your hands on the handlebars, or keep them clearly in view, and remain straddled on your bike until the officer approaches you. If you're wearing a helmet, especially a full-coverage helmet, remove it and set it down.

Wait until the officer asks for the required items: license (with endorsement), registration, and proof of insurance (in states where required), before retrieving them. Have the documents handy, ready for speedy display. Make it easy for the cop to like you, or at least, don't give him a reason to dislike you. If you have to get off your bike and dig through your junk-filled saddlebags to find your paperwork, that ups the risk to the officer and causes delays—he won't like that.

I understand that while most folks keep their licenses in their wallets, registration documents can be a bit bulky for a wallet. Find somewhere else to keep them, but I'd still suggest keeping them readily available as well. I keep my registration in a leather dash pouch on my 2005 Heritage Softail Classic™, sealed in two ziplock plastic bags. Some bikes have compartments for documents under the seat. That's fine. But if that's your situation, wait until the officer asks for the documents and then explain where they are before retrieving them. Don't make any sudden moves into concealed places. You never know if, in roll call that morning, the officer may have learned of a cop who was killed or injured by a motorcyclist who'd retrieved a weapon from within a false compartment on his bike.

The officer may instead choose for you to leave your documents within the compartment and run your registration in his computer if he has that capability, or he may call it in over the radio.

I'm laying this out methodically because I'm thinking about a motorcyclist I stopped years ago who broke all of these rules. I pulled him over for running a stop sign. When I hit my lights he darted to the side of the road, parked his bike, and jumped off the bike. He ripped his helmet off like it had a swarm of bees in it. We were on an incline and gravity can really be a bummer on motorcycles. Before I'd even gotten completely out of my car, the bike had slid backward, the kickstand scraping along the asphalt. He caught the bike before it went over, but his helmet lost its grip and dropped to the pavement and began to roll down the street, changing direction each time an open portion of the helmet made contact with the road. It rolled just slightly more predictably than a football. I could see the rider actually considering dropping his bike to retrieve the helmet. Finally, it took a benign bounce and came to rest between two parked cars, about thirty feet down the street.

The rider was incredibly nervous, and that nervousness transferred to me and my partner. We figured that he was going to have a problem with his license: either suspended or revoked, or perhaps he had a warrant for his arrest. Surprisingly, he had a good license with motorcycle endorsement and a good driving history. He had no warrant out for his arrest, no criminal history—in fact, there was no reason we could find that would cause him to act this way.

Apparently he was naturally a nervous person. He hadn't intended, by his chaotic behavior, to give us any trouble. In fact, he seemed to be overly concerned with trying to please us. Unfortunately, his behavior caused him to career in the opposite direction. Instead, he made us wary and concerned for our safety due to his unpredictable and frenetic manner. In this particular case, the motorcyclist was so freaked out that we chose to give him a break despite his behavior, but I can see, with a less-patient officer, that he might have earned himself a ticket by acting in such a way.

Once again it comes down to common sense. Put yourself in the officer's place. Between the two of you, only *you* know whether or not you intend him harm. The officer doesn't know your intentions, and he's going to be on edge until he has more information. Don't be too friendly, either; it can come off as smarmy and ingratiating and can also put an officer on guard. Just be yourself (unless you're normally a jerk; then follow my earlier tip and try to pretend you're not one for five minutes).

Here are a couple examples of motorcyclist behavior. If you choose to follow either of these, you'll take the possibility of getting off with a warning right out of the equation.

I was driving from a side street to an arterial when I observed a motorcyclist driving past. As I pulled out, I watched him punch the accelerator and begin to slalom in his lane, swerving from side to side and riding partially into the adjacent lane. He was riding a newer model Japanese motorcycle with a rear tire so wide it would have fit on a monster truck. He'd been swerving for half a block when I lit him up. He pulled over, shut the bike down, dismounted, and leaned back against the seat. He crossed his legs and folded his arms across his chest.

"You probably know why I pulled you over, right?" I said.

"No. Why?"

"You're kidding me. The way you were weaving back and forth in the lane like that?"

"Oh, that."

"Yes, that."

"I had to do that."

"Oh really. Why?"

"These are new tires so they're slick. You have to ride like this when they're new to break the tread in, to get better traction."

"Oh yeah? Can you show me that in your owner's manual?"

"These weren't the original tires."

"So, if I call the tire dealer he's going to tell me that they told you to swerve all over the road to break in your new tires?"

"No. They won't say that," the rider conceded.

"Swerving like that was your idea, then?" I asked.

"No. Everybody who rides knows you have to do that."

"Really? Hmmm . . . I ride a motorcycle to work every day. Wait right here, sir; I'll be right back."

On another occasion a motorcyclist, who had apparently not seen my patrol car, pulled out of a driveway as I was approaching and blasted down the residential road at a high rate of speed. I took off after him, lights and sirens. It took me about a mile to catch up to him. I estimated his speed at between 60 and 70 mph in a 30-mph zone. The rider was very polite and had no excuses to offer, but remember my secret formula: It's hard to argue that riding at twice the speed limit was unintentional. His dangerous behavior had also ensured that a warning was out of the question. When I asked the rider why he was riding like that, he said, "You mean, like an idiot?"

I nodded.

"Because it's fun," he said.

The rider seemed like a good guy who was being honest, but he hadn't given me anything to work with to earn a chance to get off with a warning. Now I'd be dishonest if I didn't admit that riding a motorcycle fast *is* fun. I know it is (I mean, I *imagine* it is), but it can also be very dangerous, and like other fun stuff, it can be stupid. Even in the best of circumstances—like on an official track in a sanctioned race—riding fast on two wheels is risky. No officer is likely to issue a warning to even the most pleasant of riders under the above circumstances.

If you put the advice I've provided in this chapter—and throughout this book—into practice, the officer will appreciate it. You might still get a ticket, but you won't be any worse off for being respectful, and you can feel good about yourself as a human being. (The previous sentence is spoken in a soft, FM-radio voice.) You were going about your day and you made a mistake. The officer's just going about his day, which is calling you on that mistake. Demonstrate that you understand the officer's responsibilities and his unique position, and if the officer's inclined to, you just might get off with that warning after all.

YOUR ORAL WARNING:

"I received a traffic complaint about a young, white male throwing rocks at cars passing through a neighborhood. Upon arrival, I observed a kid—approximately seven-and-a-half years old—throwing stones at anything that moved, including me on my police motorcycle. After dismounting, apprehending the criminal, and advising him of his rights, I asked, 'What's your name?' He said, 'My mom said not to talk to strangers!' and walked away."

—Sgt. P. Johns, Pompano Police Department, Georgia

CHAPTER 21

No Good Deed Goes Unpunished

"Okay, you were going fifteen over the limit, you don't have your license, and your headlight is out—but I'm just gonna give you a warning."
"Ugh, a written one?"

In this chapter . . .

☑ Most cops *do* have hearts

☑ Cut an officer some slack

☑ The "pay it forward" (or backwards) effect

You can't please everyone—so why try?

Officers know this all too well. You go the extra mile for someone or hold back on enforcing the law to the degree you probably should have, just to have it blow back into your face. Yes, sometimes doing a good deed is like peeing into the wind—on a breezy day. It's a strange phenomenon that sometimes it's the people we help the most, or for whom we most go out of our way to help, who turn around and take a big chunk out of our butts. I'm not sure what causes this behavior in some folks. Perhaps they see the officer's attempt to show them leniency as a sign of weakness, and they seek to exploit it. I'm not certain, but that's as good an explanation as I can offer.

Before I got into police work, I owned a small landscape design and construction company. I remember one client for whom my business partner and I had gone out of our way, meeting each one of her considerably fussy requirements. By the end of the ordeal, even after our extra efforts (including a discount), she refused to pay her bill, and, adding insult to nonpayment, reported us to the Better Business Bureau. We'd never had a problem like this with a client, and there was no client we'd tried as hard to make happy. Getting into police work quickly showed me that cops are certainly not immune to such incidents.

Officer Leonard Mackey sits in his patrol car on Madrona Drive, looking out on a sparkling Lake Washington on a sunny summer Sunday morning. He thinks about the upcoming Seafair events and looks forward to watching the U.S. Navy's Blue Angels as they carve up the sky with their mind-bending aerial ballet. The hydro races will be on deck below, waiting for the last jet to disappear before blasting their own contrails—or in their case, rooster tails—across the lake. Mackey looks at the water and imagines what it must be like to skip along the water, like the smooth, flat stones he used to throw across the pond back home when he was a kid, but at more than a hundred miles an hour. *Whoosh!*

Right on cue, a green minivan screams past his patrol car, interrupting his reverie. Mackey puts what's left of his spilled coffee into the holder and jets after the speeding mom-mobile. He catches up to it at the bottom of the hill where Madrona Drive intersects Lake Washington Boulevard, lights it up, and chirps his siren. The minivan pulls into the empty bus stop at the base of the T-intersection.

As Mackey approaches he can see the motorist is a woman in her late thirties with dark hair, and wearing athletic clothing. Mackey suspects she's headed for a jog on the running trail along the lake. He can also see she's sitting upright and rigid, clutching the steering wheel so hard it seems she might snap it in half.

"Good morning, ma'am. The reason I stopped you today is your speed. You passed me up the hill a ways, and all I saw and heard was a dark-green blur and a loud whoosh as you flew by me. I thought maybe the Blue Angels had arrived early. I had to accelerate to 50 miles per hour just to catch up to you all the way down here."

"Oh," is the woman's only response. She doesn't seem scared or nervous; she seems angry.

"Is there any reason for your excessive speed? A medical emergency, maybe?" Mackey offers up his routine questions.

"No." The woman hasn't moved. Mackey doesn't think he's even seen her blink.

"Ma'am, have I said or done something to offend you?"

"No."

"Could I please see your license and proof of insurance?"

The woman digs with military precision into her purse, plucks her license from her wallet, her proof of insurance from the glove compartment, and shoots her hand out the window as crisp as any buck private ever saluted a brigadier general. Her eyes never divert from her straight-ahead stare.

"Ma'am, I gotta ask you . . . Has an officer offended you, or have you had some other bad experience with the police that is making you so hostile toward me today?"

"No."

"Okay," Mackey says with a sigh. "I'll be right back."

Mackey returns to his car and begins to run the woman's driving record. She's had no collisions or violations for at least the past five years. Her violation and attitude have given Mackey every reason to write the citation, but something nags at him. He can't help feeling she's had some run-in with an officer that has turned her against all officers.

Mackey returns to the minivan. The woman appears not to

have moved an inch since he left her window. Mackey decides to try to break the ice once more.

"Ma'am, are you sure there's nothing that's happened between you and the police that is causing you to be so uncivil to me while I'm treating you with respect?"

"There's nothing; where do I sign?" she asks, still facing forward like the Sphinx.

"Well, ma'am, against my better judgment, I'm going to go ahead and let you off with a warning today. I don't know what kind of bad experience you've had with the police, but I'd like to show you that not all cops are like the one you may have met up with in the past."

"Fine. Can I go now?"

"Yes, you're free to go, but—" Before Mackey could follow his *but*, she darted off, northbound along the lake. She never did look back.

At first Mackey feels bad about giving her the warning; he thinks he's made a mistake. But the more he thinks about it, the more he decides to trust his intuition that he's done the right thing. Like the whole transaction has been some evening up of a karmic debt. He drives back up to his perch and again loses himself in the affairs of the lake.

Later, back at the station where Mackey has come in for lunch, Sergeant Wong calls him into his office.

"Hey, Len, you gotta sec?" the sergeant asks.

"For you, Sarge, always—what's up?" Mackey sits down in the chair next to Sergeant Wong's desk.

"Did you stop a lady earlier today—down by the lake?"

Mackey hesitates for a moment. He doesn't recall any traffic stops.

". . . Oh, wait a minute. Yeah, a green minivan speeding down Madrona. Yep, I remember her. How could I forget; I don't think she said five words during the stop. I got the impression she don't like cops too good."

"You're telling me," Sergeant Wong says.

"What do you mean? Why are you asking me about her?"

"You say anything to offend her?"

"Hell no. In fact, I bent over backwards to try to find out why she seemed to have something against cops. You should've seen her—stared straight ahead the whole time. Never even looked at me."

"Well, she was offended by something you did. What did you write her for?"

"I didn't write her at all, but now I'm sure wishing I had. I don't know; it's a nice day and I was in a good mood, I figured I'd try to give her a better view of the police than she obviously had— so much for my good deed for the day."

"She wanted to beef you to Internal Investigations."

"To IIS? For what? I didn't even write her."

"She says you were rude."

Mackey's chair could no longer hold him; he stood up sputtering. "I, you—I mean—how? See; how many times have I told myself, or one of my student officers: No good deed goes unpunished. What happens now? They gonna waste the taxpayers' money to investigate this BS?"

"Nope. She's satisfied that I'm gonna slap you down for your rude behavior. This won't be going to IIS."

"Well, that's something. Man, just try and be a nice guy to some folks. I won't be making that mistake again." Mackey begins to walk out of the sergeant's office.

"Hey, Len," Sergeant Wong interrupts Mackey's exit.

"Yeah?"

"Get your act together, will you. I'm tired of cleaning up all your Dirty Harry coppin'," Wong says with a smile.

"Yeah right, Sarge. That's me all right—Dirty Harry. More like, I don't know—Lethargic Lenny?"

●
●
●

After hearing this story (one that's more common than you might imagine), do you think your chances of getting a warning from this officer if he ever stops you have improved, or have become more remote? Yeah, I think that too. We're often our own worst enemies. I don't know what that woman's problem was. Maybe she doesn't like cops for no good reason, or maybe she has a really good reason, or maybe she's just nutty. Whatever the case, it illustrates the driver doing everything but spitting in the officer's eye to cause him to write her a citation, while the officer bends over backward to let a motorist off with a warning. Then the woman compounds the insult by filing a frivolous complaint against the officer. Now this woman may not care about the next motorist down the road who may have to deal with this officer, but you should.

> ☑ **Blue Light Bulletin:** Your behavior during a traffic stop has an effect on how an officer may treat the next person he stops.

Your disrespect and bad mood may cause that officer to issue tickets instead of warnings for the rest of his shift; or, perhaps in future similar circumstances, for the rest of his career. How likely is it that Officer Mackey is going to give a warning to the next motorist who acts like the woman in the green minivan did? Not likely at all, I'd say.

And another thing . . .

Police officers, deputies, troopers, and law enforcement officers in general are under more scrutiny than ever. It seems that if one of us is seen walking on water, the headlines in next day's newspapers will read: COP CAN'T SWIM! We're being held to impossible standards of behavior, and many fringe benefits we once enjoyed because of our unique and special position are slowly being eroded.

By fringe benefits I don't mean just complimentary cups of

coffee and extra sprinkles on our doughnuts. I'm talking about the respect for police officers that used to be much more automatic in our society. Cops were held in an esteem befitting the sacrifices made and risks they're willing to take to serve their communities.

Here's an apt example: In my jurisdiction, officers used to be allowed to ride public transit for free, in or out of uniform, the tacit understanding being that if something illegal occurred, the officer would be there to take action. In a recent change, officers may now only ride for free if they're in uniform. So, that immediately dissuades non-uniformed officer positions and detectives from riding buses, making the public less safe. As for uniformed officers—few officers are going to want to get onto a crowded bus and sit with their backs to unknown passengers, making themselves a visible target.

Local law enforcement officers aren't allowed to be armed when testifying in Federal Court. (Bet you didn't know that. I sure didn't until they took my gun.) Local law enforcement officers aren't allowed to be armed on commercial airlines. What do you think? Does that make you safer or put you more at risk?

Officers all over the country watch the news, and it seems almost nightly a fellow officer somewhere is being accused of abusing someone's rights. We watch replay after replay and are oftentimes left saying: "So what? I do that all the time. It's the way I was taught." Of course it doesn't look good on TV, especially when the same ten-second clip, showing the officer's response only, is played over and over, while what the suspect had done to initiate that response is rarely, if ever, played.

The video shows the big, strong officer slamming the poor, helpless suspect down on the hood of his car. The officer looks enraged and out of control; the suspect looks vulnerable and scared. Well, right, he should be scared. I'd be scared too if I'd just grabbed the big, strong officer's crotch, clamped down, and twisted. Would you be able to think clearly and remain professionally detached at such a moment? Speaking, at least for the male half of the population, I think not. If I were that suspect I wouldn't be surprised if I suddenly became a hood ornament.

A suspect is not subdued or under control, even if he's in handcuffs, until all the resisting has ceased. Handcuffed suspects have escaped, taken hostages, stolen police cars, and even killed cops. As long as the suspect continues to fight, officers have to work quickly and efficiently to bring him under control. Sometimes this means additional force, additional restraints, and perhaps spit masks. (I reserve an extreme dislike for spitters and biters.)

Again, it may seem that we're going far afield from our original discussion, but I assure you we're not—really. I want you to get a broader picture of why cops act the way they do, and why sometimes they seem a bit gruff. In instances like the green minivan story above, sometimes they take the opposite approach by going out of their way to try to show a motorist that not all cops are jerks, as the motorist seems to believe. Whether the tactic works or not—I suspect, sometimes yes; sometimes no—still, some of us continue, on occasion, to try. Maybe it'll bring good karma.

At any rate, cops are under intense scrutiny and are often frivolously accused of excessive force, abusing authority, and all sorts of pillaging and mayhem, often for political and vindictive purposes. It sure makes for great headlines, and while a small percentage of cops do abuse their authority, most of us are out here trying to make our communities a safer place for people to live and work.

Now to come, as they say, full circle: Yes, I do have a point related to getting warnings here, rather than citations, and, I promise, I am getting to it. As an officer it's hammered into us that if it's not written down, it didn't happen. We get injured—there better be an injury report documenting the specific circumstances. We use force in an arrest—we'd better have filed the correct reports and forms documenting the incident, including taking any photographs. Oh yes, it's very important that we carefully document even the remotest and slightest possibility that a suspect might have been injured.

As for cops who are assaulted in the line of duty, often the "system" is less than diligent with prosecutions.

I know of no jurisdiction where assaulting an officer while in the commission of his duties is not a felony. However, in some jurisdictions, simple assaults against a law enforcement officer are more often prosecuted as misdemeanors, thus weakening the intent of the law. Now, before I move on, some folks may wonder why it should be a felony to simply strike a police officer, when it's a misdemeanor to strike the average person.

There is a very important reason: Police officers are the sword arm of society. We're not out here wearing targets on our chests and taking abuse from the worst criminals Hades ever secreted because we relish rolling in the gutter with these vermin; we're out here for you. We act on your behalf. When a suspect strikes a police officer, they are striking at the very thing that has been put in place to keep society civil and operating smoothly. The police allow people to pursue their happiness.

You remember the story of the whacked-out brother with the multiple knives on him? He threatened to kill me and several other officers with his weapons. He said he didn't care that we were the police; he was going to kill us anyway. Well, I got called into the prosecutor's office to discuss the case and was told point-blank that the state wasn't going to charge the suspect with the assaults on, and threats to, kill a police officer. Let's see if I can remember his words correctly, or at least the gist of them: "It's a part of your job, Officer."

Stopping assaults is a part of my job, not inviting them. Between officers suffering a barrage of unwarranted accusations and with police administrations and the justice system marginalizing law enforcement officers and eroding our discretion in the field, is it any wonder that cops are cautious?

An oral warning to a traffic violator is an important tool to the law enforcement officer, but if my department is any indication of a trend, the day of the oral warning may be coming to a close. We lost this tool a few years ago based upon two arguments: One was to conduct a "Racial Profiling" study, which at the time of this writing is apparently lost in some mysterious bureaucratic abyss. But, then again, it seems that every time they do one of these studies on a law enforcement agency, they come up empty for systemic or institutional racial profiling. I suppose our detractors will continue trying and manipulating the data until they get the results they want. The second argument was, as I mentioned above, to protect the officer by creating a written document for each contact, even minor ones such as traffic warnings.

By taking away an officer's discretion to issue an oral warning, you're making things more difficult for any motorist hoping for a warning. When a department takes away the oral warning and instead forces, by policy, the officer to issue written warnings only, the officer is left with an interesting choice. Prior to the policy change the officer felt free to make a "quick" traffic stop for educational purposes, maybe on the way to a low-priority call. A brief stop to tell a motorist to signal next time, wish her a nice day, then be back on his way to the original call. But now the officer is much more inclined to write you a ticket; a ticket that counts as a higher stat for documenting purposes than a written warning. In fact, a written warning counts no more than an oral warning did; it just involves more time and labor.

Given that once the officer has stopped you, he is now mandated to write you something, warning or ticket, which one do you think it's going to be more prudent for him to write? Hell, he's got to write anyway; he may as well make it count.

It also affects officer-motorist relations in that the oral warning is friendly and informal. It takes a short amount of time, and more often than not the violator actually appears almost happy to have been stopped. It fosters good relations; but then again, the folks that make those decisions and rules don't actually deal with the motorists on a day-to-day basis; cops do.

Now when it comes to issuing warnings at all, I've already said that my agency doesn't issue oral warnings, so for us, it's written warning or ticket. This piece of advice is for those of you dealing with agencies whose leadership remains enlightened, or hasn't succumbed to the pressure—at least as it pertains to oral warnings. An oral warning is an undocumented transaction—one I'd argue is still valuable—but one that others may argue is outdated in our litigious culture.

When an officer chooses to issue you an oral warning, there's a sort of trust going on there. He has to believe that you are sorry for the infraction you've committed, you understand why it was wrong, and you appreciate the warning. Because in a situation where an oral warning becomes a dispute—when a person the officer intends to warn decides that he didn't like getting stopped after all—the officer will have no choice but to write the motorist a citation to document the incident. Like it says in this chapter's title: *No good deed . . .*

A situation like this becomes your word against his or her word; the classic "he said, she said." These incidents are hard to prove one way or the other, and officers often don't enjoy the benefit of the doubt they once did. Written warnings aren't much better, but at least there is something written down at the time of the incident.

So, if an officer who's about to issue an oral warning begins to suspect in the slightest that the motorist might be complaint-prone, kiss that warning good-bye. If he's concerned that you may file a complaint against him despite having issued you an oral warning, he's probably not even going to issue a written warning. Instead, he's going to do what I would do in that case: issue a citation. A citation is a legal charging document upon which an officer is basically swearing out an affidavit to the facts of the case. This obviously has much more weight than a warning of any kind.

There you have it: You want a ticket instead of a warning, then give the officer a reason to suspect that you intend to file a complaint against him. In fact, in that case you've put the officer in the position where he *has* to give you a ticket. Remember what I said: *Once stopped, you've already earned the ticket.* The officer who's issuing you a warning can change his mind at any time and decide to issue you a citation instead.

Well, you've had admin types passing policies that make your odds of getting off with a warning more difficult, and you've just heard about a lady who's driving around sabotaging your chances after receiving a warning. Is that enough to piss you off? Yeah? Hopefully not too angry that it affects your driving. Ever hear of road rage? Ever experience road rage? The answers to both of these questions is, undoubtedly, yes. Good. Let's move on to the next chapter and discuss that issue for a while. Might just calm us down a bit.

YOUR ORAL WARNING:

"I really don't mind hearing a good excuse. Just do it with a smile and at least make it entertaining. Who knows? It may get you out of a ticket and make it into a book one day."

—Sergeant T. Nicosia, Las Vegas Police Department (retired)

CHAPTER 22

Road Rage–Grrrr!

".. . Doing just fine, Officer. And yourself?"

In this chapter . . .

☑ Don't get sucked in by a jerk

☑ Remember what Mom taught you: Count to ten

☑ The consequences of losing control on the road

Grit 'em and bear it:

I couldn't write a book about how to act in ways that will up your chances of getting off with a warning rather than getting a ticket without mentioning the phenomenon of *road rage*—Da-da-daaaaa! (Insert ominous music.) I say phenomenon not because of the idiots out there for whom road rage is a constant state of being while behind the wheel or handlebars, but because of how this destructive behavior can infect even the best of motorists.

One note about road rage: This is not a new phenomenon; it's always been with us. To paraphrase ABC TV *20/20*'s John Stossel from his book, *Myths, Lies, and Downright Stupidity*, while our mass media seems to have an affection for the alliterative flow of the phrase, there's probably no more "rage" than there's ever been; it's just that now, we have a cool name for it. Regardless of what we call it, and for lack of a better term, *road rage* works as well as anything to describe the behaviors that cause stress and danger on the roads.

Also, and this is important, if you exhibit road rage during a traffic incident, even if the other motorist who drove off started it, you're going to substantially decrease your chances of getting off with a warning. For one thing, you're likely to be highly emotional from the anger you're carrying for the other motorist. It would be easy in this state to transfer your anger to the officer, and even if you apologize afterward, the warning ship is likely to have already sailed over the horizon. Remember, the officer will be calm and will have a hard time understanding or empathizing with your rage while he's investigating your incident.

If the circumstances were right, I think even Mother Teresa might have been sucked into that black hole known as road rage, which can cause even the most serene of us to behave in ways outside of our normal personality. Our vehicles seem to give us a sense of invulnerability. My wife is a good example of this effect, although her rage has been limited to loud expletives and obscene gestures—so far no physical violence of which I am aware. (Well, except for her tendency to back-slap me in the chest if I'm not sufficiently offended by what she's just endured.)

I've warned her again and again that I'm not particularly interested in engraving on her headstone: HERE LIES A SMART WOMAN WHO, HER ANGER HAVING GOTTEN THE BEST OF HER, DID A STUPID THING AND NOW HER CHILDREN HAVE NO MOTHER AND HER HUSBAND HAS NO WIFE.

I've waxed (quasi-) serious here, because I've seen what can happen when a normally decent person expresses road rage toward the wrong motorist. Hell, there've been instances where both parties are normally law-abiding, and now one's dead and the other's in prison, both having left families behind to celebrate anniversaries, graduations, and weddings without them. When your mother taught you to count to ten when angry, she was right. Take that advice along with a deep breath; it's simply not worth the alternative.

Grit your teeth, breathe deeply; make a game of it if you have to. It's far easier to let loose your rage on another motorist than it is to contain or dismiss it entirely. Challenge yourself to be strong and not surrender to your weakness. Any idiot can scream and drive like a maniac bent on retaliation. It takes a strong person to resist this powerful urge to even the score. In a road-rage incident, there can be one stupid party or there can be two; it's your choice.

At times we may feel invincible, but we're not:

We get angry when people put us and our loved ones at risk. When you're driving along in your car and someone tailgates you with their two or three thousand or more pounds of vehicle, the significance of the threat can't help but push your "anger" button. Perhaps you have the kids in the backseat at the time, which is all the more reason to back off and change lanes. It's bad enough when this danger sparks our ire, but often it's merely the fact that our egos have been tweaked that gets us fired up. Someone cuts us off, goes out of turn at a four-way stop, or takes *our* parking space. I'll tell you right now, there's no law against being a jerk, and you won't be surprised to hear me say that the jails would be bursting at their seams if there were. Just let it go.

Believe me; I'm no different than you when it comes to road rage. I've found myself gritting my teeth more than once, and found my ego pushed and prodded a time or two, or a dozen. This is particularly true when I'm riding my motorcycle, and especially when my wife is with me. Glancing in my rearview mirrors while riding my eight-hundred-pound Harley-Davidson and seeing a multi-ton truck so close to my taillight it looks like I'm pulling the rig as a trailer, would be enough to seal up anyone's butt cheeks. I'm fearful of the imminent threat bearing down behind me, threatening what I hold most dear in life—and on top of that, my wife's riding on the passenger seat!

But seriously folks, tell me how is this any different than having someone running behind you with a shotgun pointed at your head with his finger on the trigger? He's probably not going to trip, causing his finger to flex, depressing the trigger and putting buckshot in the back of your head, but he wouldn't *for sure* if he'd just take his finger off that trigger! It's the same deal with the idiot in the truck. He wouldn't be a threat if he'd simply back off to a safe distance. And like I mentioned before, whether you're sixty feet, or six inches, behind the car in front of you, you're not going to get there any quicker. Okay, maybe fifty-nine feet, six inches quicker.

When I find myself in a potential road-rage situation, I slap handcuffs on my ego and simply change lanes and let the slimy vermin pass by on the way to his rat's den and trust that karma will serve up a heaping helping of justice—truly appropriate justice—at another time. Sometimes you just have to trust the universe, your gods, or God (I want to cover all my bases) to slam on the divine brakes in front of the tailgating moron like you wanted to do so badly.

Off-road (and off-the-rocker) raging:

Now there's road rage, and then there's—well, I'll let you decide for yourself what to call this next incident.

My partner and I were on routine patrol, minding our own business, our virtual blinders in place (actually, we were headed to Starbucks), when . . .

"You see that?" I asked.

"Yeah; I think we're gonna need to have a chat with her," my partner said as he reached down and flipped on the toggle switch for the overheads. I whipped the car around and caught up to the violator in a short distance; speed wasn't the issue.

"Good afternoon, ma'am. The reason I stopped you is you failed to yield to oncoming traffic when you pulled out of the gas station; you could have caused a collision," I said.

The short-cropped, salt-and-pepper-haired woman, who appeared to be in her late fifties, sat silently in her maroon Toyota Camry, her hands clutching the steering wheel. Her face was expressionless.

"I also noticed that your tabs expired two months ago, ma'am," I added.

She slowly turned her head and looked at me. Her eyes were intense; she seemed to be making one eye larger than the other, with one brow arched high into her forehead and the other dipped in a sinister swoop. She turned her head toward the other side of her car, her expression reversed, with the opposite eyes dipping and swooping, she stared at my partner for a moment. Then her expression returned to its original configuration as she slowly turned her fierce glare back toward me.

"Ma'am, I need to see your license and proof of insurance, please," I said, the hairs on the back of my neck standing erect like new grass in springtime.

"You don't need to see anything from me."

"Um, actually I do."

"No."

"No?" I looked over to my partner. He looked back, conveying to me that he was happy it was me dealing with her and not him.

"Ma'am, it's against the law to refuse to provide me with your license and insurance information when I ask for it."

"No."

"Ma'am, I've been through this before. Let me tell you how it goes. You say, 'no,' I call my supervisor to the scene. If you continue to say no to him, you could be charged with a crime—in fact, you could actually end up in jail. Doesn't it seem silly to go to jail over something like this?"

"Yes it does. So why don't you just let me go and stop ruining my day?" Her voice began to rise to an almost screeching level by the end of the sentence. *This did not bode well for us.*

"I'm sorry, ma'am; I can't do that. It's my job to enforce the traffic laws, and what you did was very dangerous."

"I didn't even hit anyone. What's the matter with you? You're ruining my whole day. You know that? You're ruining my whole day!" She was becoming unhinged, shaking, and grabbing her steering wheel like she was trying to snap it off its column, which I wasn't so sure she couldn't do if she kept it up.

"Ma'am, please calm down," I said.

"Calm down? Calm down? Why don't *you* calm down and leave me the hell alone? Stop ruining my day." She pounded her steering wheel with both fists, wrapped both hands around it again and began to squeeze it—her fingers turning white as she gritted her teeth. Then she actually began growling. I stood silent for a moment, hoping the pause would help to calm her down. Distance must have been some sort of amulet casting a force field of sorts, as my partner's body began to shake with mirth as I suffered the onslaught of this—I'll be nice—woman.

I suppose I could have just left, but two things prevented me from doing so: One, I was afraid to send her back into traffic in her agitated state; and two, this sort of behavior shouldn't be rewarded. It wouldn't be fair to only penalize those who cooperated with the police and let those who didn't get off scot-free.

"Ma'am? Are you calm now? I need to see your license."

She reached into her glove compartment and retrieved a proof-of-insurance card. She dug into her purse and plucked out her license. She emitted a low growl as she slapped the documents into my chest.

"Uh, thank you, ma'am."

"Just get this over with—now." She slapped her steering wheel.

"I'll be right back. Please remain in your car, ma'am."

I returned to our patrol car and wrote out a citation. As I wrote, my partner kept an eye on this unpredictable driver, barely able to contain his amusement. We could see her flailing in her car, talking to herself—obviously still quite agitated.

I returned to her car. She watched me in her side-view mirror the entire way as I approached. She'd calmed down and was staring at me, having reacquired her cockeyed glare. I remember thinking that she was giving me the evil eye; I'd never been on the receiving end of an evil eye except for my wife's, which was Irish-flavored. I'd soon find out that my sense of her intent wasn't too far off. I handed her the ticket book and my pen. She took it and signed the citation without a word. I took the book back and gave her the copy of her ticket as I explained to her the court instructions. I was relieved that she'd apparently resigned herself to the situation.

And then I asked if she had any questions.

Spell check:

"Questions? Questions? No, I don't have any questions for you; you ruined my day. But I do have something for you," she said as she raised her right hand up ceremoniously and pointed two crooked fingers at me. "I hex you. I hex you," she incanted. "I hex you. There, I've put a hex on you, and I hope it ruins your whole day." Then she put her car in gear and drove off in a remarkably controlled huff.

For the second time in my career—the first had been a quick parting shot—I was on the receiving end of a hex; well, there may have been others, but if so, I wasn't aware of them. I use this story to demonstrate that road rage can come from people from whom we least expect it, and in the most unexpected ways. This event certainly ended better than having someone pull out a Glock and empty its fourteen-round magazine (and one in the chamber) into my car—but who knows what damage her hex has done over the years?

●
●
●

People experience and demonstrate road rage in many different ways. First, we all may react differently to the same event. For instance, I'm in my patrol car for nine hours a day up to my neck in instances that incite road rage, such as tailgating and failure-to-yield violations. So when I drive my personal car, I tend to be more forgiving of other vehicles. Not because I excuse their driving, but because it preserves my sanity to ignore it as much as possible when I'm off-duty. This drives my firefighter wife, who's used to muscling her way through traffic in a massive fire engine, absolutely nuts. So I just let her curse and gesture for the both of us, while making sure I have easy access to my off-duty weapon—just in case.

Being a passenger doesn't even stop her from getting a little, well, *ragey*.

"Oh, I knew that guy was going to cut you off," she says as we're driving northbound on Interstate 5.

"What do you mean, 'cut me off'? He was practically in Canada," I said.

Her buttons are obviously a smidge more sensitive than mine. If I impress nothing else upon you about road rage, remember this: Count to ten, pretend you aren't offended, and don't let some lowlife drag you into something from which you can't safely extract yourself.

YOUR ORAL WARNING:

"I pay your salary. It was yellow. I want your badge number. I'm calling my attorney. Anything like that and I would guess a potential warning might turn into a citation pretty fast."

—Officer M. Wong, Seattle Police Department, Patrol

CHAPTER 23

A Hot Date—in Court

Innocent until proven guilty . . . or the pen runs out.

In this chapter . . .

☑ Choices you have

☑ People to contact and costs to pay

☑ What to expect while in court

I got a ticket anyway—now what?

So you've heeded my advice, but despite your angelic smile and saintly demeanor, instead of a warning, the officer socked you with a ticket. You might be thinking: *What good is this flatfoot's advice anyway?* Well, my answer is, how about next time you slow the heck down or actually stop for that bloody red light? Just kidding; like I said before, *other* cops make occasional mistakes and karma just may be exacting payment for some unrelated indiscretion from you. Regardless, I'm not going to judge you—not my job; in fact you can depend on me to keep helping you.

One way I won't help you, though, is by providing any advice on how to "beat" the system. If you want to try that, you're on your own. Remember I said that once you've committed the infraction, you've earned it? I meant that. At any rate, courts are so unpredictable these days that I've stopped trying to predict how things will go on a criminal case, never mind a traffic ticket.

Some judges are sticklers for details, while other judges know that 99.9 percent of the people standing before them did what the officer said they did and deserved the ticket. Some judges will dismiss a ticket if the language is not exact on the ticket, while others understand that mistakes happen. Some judges will dismiss the ticket if the officer doesn't show up, while other judges will find it sufficient and rely solely on the officer's written narrative on the citation. In other words, even if I wanted to give you "insider" info on how to "beat" a ticket, it would remain a crapshoot anyway—unless you want to hire a lawyer, which would cost you much more than the ticket.

Every state has its own specific procedures for processing traffic citations. However, the options for handling tickets are similar throughout the United States. I'm providing information based upon the procedures followed in the City of Seattle and the State of Washington, with which I am most familiar. With few exceptions, if any, the advice should be applicable with little modification in every state.

Many, if not most, court jurisdictions now have Internet sites that provide detailed information on how to handle traffic tickets. You can also telephone your local traffic court and they will assist you with any questions you may have about the process. If you're in a *Hawaii 5-0* mood, you can also surf the Web, where you'll find several sites from around the nation that deal with the court process regarding citations.

Since this book's primary focus is on how to increase your chances of getting a warning at the time of the stop, the above information should be sufficient.

Once cited, you'll have two basic options to handle the citation: Pay the fine, or fight the ticket in court. In Washington State there is a third option (your state may have this too): You can request a mitigation hearing. In a mitigation hearing the driver admits to having committed the violation, but offers evidence showing a legitimate reason for having done so, or compelling mitigating circumstances. A mitigating circumstance could be something like bright sunlight obscuring your vision.

> ☑ **Blue Light Bulletin:** If you decide to fight the Man, let's talk about what you can expect, depending on which option you choose. When you decide to fight a ticket, you must be painfully honest with yourself. Be certain that your reasoning is not mucked up in denial.

A few days removed from the emotion of the incident, ask yourself the question, *Did I commit the infraction?* Come on—be honest. I'm not talking about whether or not you feel that you deserved a warning, but did you actually do what the officer is accusing you of doing? If yes, then for your own peace of mind . . . I don't want to tell you what to do here, but perhaps you should just go ahead and pay the ticket and move on with your life.

For one thing, should you choose to fight the ticket, the judge isn't very likely to care if you're a good person, a fellow Capricorn, it was your birthday, or you think you deserved a break. To put it bluntly: If you can't logically debunk the officer's proof, you're sunk. Once you get into court, the standard is: Based upon the evidence, is it more likely than not you committed the infraction. Well, unless you've got a videotape showing unequivocally that you didn't commit the violation, and since you won't be able to retain Johnnie Cochran, who passed away in 2005, as your defense counsel (if the ticket doesn't fit, you must acquit), you're just setting yourself up for disappointment and embarrassment.

The wrong of way:

In the event that you do have a mitigation option in your jurisdiction, here's an example with which you can compare your situation. The following traffic collision involved two passenger cars and was witnessed by a school-bus operator.

"Are you okay?" I asked the apparently uninjured young woman standing beside her damaged car.

"Yes, Officer; I'm fine."

"What happened?"

"I was across from the bus, on that side." She pointed to the intersection. "I couldn't see the cars coming the other way very well. But the bus driver waved at me to go, so I went and—well, you can see," she said, pointing at her crumpled car door.

The bus had turned into a parking lot and the driver was apparently waiting to speak with officers if needed as a witness.

"Hello, ma'am. Can you tell me what you saw?" I asked the bus driver.

"I was over there across from that red car, waiting for traffic to pass so I could pull out, when it just came out in front of that black car and *wham!*" She slapped her hands on the steering wheel.

"Yeah, that part I've figured out; but the driver of the red car is telling me that you waved at her to go ahead."

"No way. I didn't do that—I don't know what she's talking about," she said, emphatically beginning to rise from her seat.

"Hold on, ma'am, I'm not accusing you of anything. I'm just trying to gather the facts for my report," I said. She calmed down and sank back into her seat.

"I'm sorry, Officer. It's been a long day."

"I understand. So you didn't wave at her—maybe you did something that looked like you were waving her on?"

"No, Officer—nothing. I was just waiting to pull out myself."

"Okay, ma'am, thank you." I started to walk away when she called me back.

"Yes, ma'am?" I strolled back over to the open folding door.

"You know what? A bee flew into the bus while I was waiting for traffic. I was trying to smack it away. She could have seen me doing that. In fact, that makes a lot of sense," she said with a smile, embarrassed.

"Yes it does. Thanks again, ma'am."

I walked back to the blonde who was talking on her cell phone while leaning against her car. She hung up and pushed away from her car.

"Insurance company?" I asked.

"Uh-huh, yeah," she nodded.

"Well, ma'am, I have some good news and some bad news. The good news is she was waving; the bad news is, not at you. She said a bee flew into her bus and was buzzing near her face. She was waving her hand, trying to slap the little bugger away."

The girl's head drooped; it obviously made sense to her too, but didn't appear to make her feel much better.

"Does that make a difference, Officer?" she asked.

"Well, it does, but not right now. You see, if possible, we're supposed to find fault according to evidence of a rules-of-the-road violation, which means a moving violation. Like, if you run a red light, or a stop sign, or fail to yield, it's your fault. On the other hand, you can't be found at fault for something administrative like your license plates having expired. Make sense?"

"Yes, I think so."

"So, in this case, the driver of the black car was driving along, minding her own business; she had the right-of-way. Unfortunately, you failed to yield the right-of-way to her, for whatever reason, when you pulled out in front of her, causing the collision. So, I have to find you at fault for my preliminary investigation and issue you a citation. Sorry."

"I understand. You said it could help me somewhere else, though?"

"Right; I always tell folks: I wasn't here; I didn't witness the collision. I encourage you to contest the ticket or, if you feel there are some mitigating circumstances, then choose a mitigation hearing. Even though in this case it was your fault, the judge may understand you weren't being careless, may sympathize with your situation, and reduce your fine. We all take advantage of others waving us on from time to time. I used to too, but not anymore. There were some reports of scumbags waving cops on at intersections and then crashing into the officer, placing the officer at fault for the collision. It's an effective tactic for insurance fraud as well. When I teach my student officers about other drivers waving them on, I know the other drivers are probably just being nice, but I warn them to never take, what I call, the *wrong* of way."

"So, you think in this case I should take it to court?" she asked.

"Well, everyone's circumstances are different. I think that you have a legitimate mitigating circumstance here, but it might not be worth taking a day off work and paying for parking downtown, just to get the ticket fine reduced. If you contested the ticket and won, that would be more worthwhile, because then the ticket wouldn't go on your record. With a mitigation hearing, the ticket still counts; you just get a break on the fine."

"You think I should contest it instead?"

"I'm not saying that. Like I said, I wasn't there, and you have the right to contest it, but the judge would have to find that you didn't fail to yield in this instance, and that's not likely—he or she would have to ignore the facts. But you never know; I've been surprised more than once by a judge's ruling. At any rate, that's your decision to make. You'll have fifteen days to send your response to the court. Talk to people, weigh the pros and cons, then make your decision. Now, could you please sign here? By signing this, you're not admitting to having committed any . . ."

Here come the judge:

If you've chosen to take your ticket to court and contest it, much of the same advice I've given you for dealing with the constabulary is also valid for the judiciary. Be polite and honest. Remember, more often than not the judge will base his or her decision on the facts of the case as they are presented, but in cases where all else is equal, your pleasant demeanor won't hurt your cause. Most often the facts are simply presented as the officer's word—his or her account of the infraction, written in a narrative on the citation and/or given by testimony in court. In some speeding cases, evidence could also include radar-gun or aircraft monitoring results.

Remember what I said about cops not having to fabricate traffic stops. The judge is aware of this too; he won't be interested in your excuses or in your bad-mouthing the officer. Chances are, especially in smaller jurisdictions, the judge knows the cops, and contrary to some public perceptions, cops do their best to earn a good reputation with judges by being honest so they can earn the benefit of the doubt on those close calls.

Just the facts, ma'am:

If you have a legitimate argument, present it, but stick to the facts of the case. Present your own evidence. Now, your evidence, just like the officer's, may simply be your testimony. That's fine, but make what you have to say count; ensure that you're making sense and not just afflicted with a case of verbal diarrhea. If you think the officer was truly wrong or mistaken, articulate specific reasons for the judge. He knows that you're not a legal professional, and he'll give you some latitude in explaining your case, but he'll have little patience with you wasting the court's time with superfluous details and silly minutiae—get to your point. If you begin to blather on about inane, arcane, and innocuous points of contention, the judge's focus is going to shift from your case to the dozens waiting for yours to finish.

Believe me; I know what I'm talking about. Not from sitting on the blue side of the courtroom, but from languishing on the lonely civilian side. Remember the story of my fighting, and losing, my own ticket battle? Well, as valid as I thought my arguments were (and still think they are), and as intent on convicting me as the judge appeared to be, upon reflection I realize that I overwhelmed the court with blather (albeit brilliant blather, but verbal diarrhea nonetheless), which clouded the basic issue: Was the State able to prove by a preponderance of empirical evidence that I'd committed the infraction? We all know my answer to that question, don't we?

I failed to take my own advice. I broadened the scope to what I now see was an absurd degree—although I remain convinced, whether I'd presented my case in two minutes or two hours, it would've made little difference.

Don't overwhelm the court:

If you have photographic evidence, keep it limited to only a few photographs. Don't overwhelm the judge with as many photographs as it would take to fill a photo album with every O'Reilly in Dublin. Ask yourself if each photo actually proves something. Just photographing your car or the scene of the infraction isn't good enough, unless the scene shows a discrepancy in the government's proof against you.

For example, and I've done this, the officer has cited you for running a stop sign at 32nd Avenue and Spring Street. You go back and photograph the intersection. Your photo shows that there is a yield sign at this intersection, not a stop sign. This is obvious proof that you didn't run a stop sign, at least not at this intersection. Maybe you violated the yield sign, but the driver's obligations at a yield sign are different from those at a stop sign, and that's not why the officer cited you. The government has the burden of proof. Your photographic evidence makes it impossible to convict you. They have no proof, unless they can show that there was a stop sign at that location at the time of the infraction and it's since been replaced with a yield sign, which isn't likely.

The search for justice may lead to disappointment:

So, there you have it; you've had your day in court. I'm not promising that you'll find the justice you seek—a romp through the American justice system can end in frustration and disappointment. To me, American justice is similar to what Winston Churchill once said about democracy: "Democracy is the worst form of Government except all those others that have been tried from time to time." Seeking justice can be a messy affair. You *know* what happened to you, but no one else is in your mind and, just as important, you're not in anyone else's. Two different perspectives are presented to the judge, and in the majority of cases the ruling is based upon objective reasoning. That reasoning may or may not find your way, but that's the chance you take. Remember, life isn't always fair, and sometimes a day in court makes that all too clear.

> ☑ **Blue Light Bulletin:** Don't let this discourage you if you truly feel that you have a case. There's nothing wrong with a quest for justice; in fact, it's admirable, and, on occasion, inspiring. So, think about the things I've told you and make your decision, but make sure you open your mind before you open your mouth.

"Hang up the cell phone and talk to me. You can call your friend, mother, husband, lawyer, whomever . . . after the stop. No kidding; I've stopped people and had them pull out their cell phones to ask for advice. . . . I've even had the other end of the phone call show up at the scene before I was done writing the ticket—to help make the violator's case for them. Since I can't put their cell phones where I would like to, I consider settling for adding the litter bag and dirty license plate fines to their citations."

—Detective T. Doran, Seattle Police Department, Burglary

CHAPTER 24

Are You Challenging Me?

"Just accept it. There's no point in fighting, man . . ."

In this chapter . . .

☑ Dealing with multiple perspectives

☑ Accidents versus collisions—there's a difference

☑ It may suck, but maybe you really *did* do it

How cops feel about motorists who fight tickets:

If you choose to contest a citation, you may be intimidated at the thought of having to confront the officer in court. You may be even more nervous if you've never fought a ticket before. Like people in general, every officer is different. Some love the overtime and don't mind going to court even on a day off. Others haul themselves reluctantly to court—even while on duty—and would rather be dragged naked through broken Christmas ornaments embedded in hot tar than go to court on their days off. I'll describe myself as somewhere in the middle.

Many officers are perfectionists with regard to issuing citations, especially if they're rookies (or are assigned to a traffic unit where traffic enforcement is a primary function). They take great pride in getting their facts straight every time. (Hopefully all cops are like this, at least to some degree.) It's a matter of pride for these officers, and some may not like their tickets challenged, considering it a personal affront; from my experience, however, this sentiment is rare. Regardless of whether or not the officer is pissed that you challenged the ticket, it won't change the fact-based reasoning of the judge. If the facts are on your side, present them honestly and without hostility.

> ☑ **Blue Light Bulletin:** Remember, regardless of the officer's view of it, you're not opposing the officer—just his perception of your specific situation.

All cops (yes, even me) make mistakes:

Most officers I know realize mistakes happen from time to time. They know this because, like any other human being, they've made them before and they'll make them again. This is especially true in a profession where many decisions have to be made in a split second. These officers don't take offense at those who attempt to contest their tickets; they realize that the defendants are simply exercising their rights.

Funny? I'll be the judge of that:

Last, but not least (and I count myself among these officers), are officers who enjoy traffic court because they find it can be a great source of humor. You don't even have to pay a cover charge for the entertainment.

The court clerk swears in the defendant. The defendant had been stopped by an officer who was aware that the defendant had no valid license. The officer had stopped him repeatedly in the past, and he'd verified the defendant's driver's status in his computer prior to pulling him over.

"But Your Honor, I wasn't driving," the frequent scofflaw testifies.

"Sir, the officer has testified that he saw you driving," the judge replies.

"He's lying, Your Honor." The man avoids looking at the officer. The officer can't help himself; a slim smirk cracks his stone face.

"What do you mean, he's lying?" the judge asks.

"He never saw me driving," the man states emphatically.

"It says right here on the ticket that he first saw you in the twenty-one-hundred block of Twenty-sixth Avenue . . ." the judge begins.

"Yes, Your Honor, that's my house," the man interrupts.

". . . and he followed you to the twenty-three-hundred block of Twenty-sixth Avenue, right?" the judge asks.

"Yes, that's my grandpa's place," he says.

"Well, sir, if you admit that you were in your car in one place when the officer first saw you, and in another place when he finally stopped you, how can you say that he didn't see you driving?" the judge asks.

"Because I wasn't driving; I was just *moving* the car from my house to Grandpa's to work on it," he finishes, with a satisfied smile on his face.

Yeah, it sucks, but sometimes it's just plain your fault:

Consider this chain-reaction collision investigation. A line of cars was stopped for a traffic light on a wide arterial, which passes through a neighborhood consisting of residences, churches, and schools. One driver didn't realize that the traffic ahead had stopped for a red light. He failed to brake in time and struck a vehicle from the rear, apparently causing that driver's foot to slip off the brake and onto the gas pedal. That car shot forward, glanced off two cars, and caused oncoming cars to swerve to avoid a head-on collision. The car then careened down the side-walk, skimming along a hedge, until it collided with a power pole, knocking it down and causing power lines to dangle precariously over the street.

The driver who'd caused the collision was a nice man. He was cooperative and immediately provided me with all the necessary documents. He even volunteered his guilt and apologized for the collision. However, as time passed and people were transported to the hospital (fortunately, no serious injuries occurred), and City Light workers arrived to address the power pole and line issue, the at-fault driver began to question whether the blame should be placed entirely on his shoulders. He asked me to consider the pos-sibility that the elderly man he'd hit from behind may have simply panicked and stepped on the gas instead of the brake—versus his foot accidentally slipping off the brake and onto the accelerator.

I told the man that could've been what happened, but there was no evidence to prove it. Since he'd struck the man's vehicle from behind, every action following was a result of his initial action. The man remained pleasant but, I sensed, not satisfied.

It is what it is:

When I saw the subpoena show up in my mailbox at work, I was somewhat intrigued that the at-fault driver had chosen to contest the citation, but not at all upset with him. Again, I hadn't witnessed the infraction, but who knows—maybe he could convince a judge that the collision wasn't entirely his fault (although I doubted it). The only thing we knew for sure was that he wasn't paying attention when he struck a man's car from the rear while it was stopped behind other cars at a red light. The elderly driver had simply been sitting behind the wheel of his car, minding his own business when he was hit.

The defendant didn't assess the situation from the officer's perspective before deciding to contest the ticket; he was relying on emotion. Yeah, it sucked that his relatively minor collision had caused such significant damage: five cars damaged, three people sent to the hospital, and a power pole and lines mowed down. But, it was what it was.

Bad advice:

I recognized the defendant when he entered the courtroom. He smiled nervously and I returned the smile, which seemed to make him relax a bit. When his case was called, surprisingly, his lawyer stood up and announced that his client had changed his mind and decided to plead guilty and pay the fine.

Outside the courtroom he came up to me, shook my hand, and apologized for "wasting my time." I told him not to worry about it. He told me that his lawyer had advised him to contest the ticket. I told him that was bad advice. He agreed. He told me that while sitting in court, he realized that the judge wasn't going to care about what he thought or felt, but would be interested in what he could prove. That's when he realized he had no proof, and decided to change his plea. I told him I respected that and wished him good luck.

Traffic court:

Remember, when it comes to traffic court—unlike criminal court, where we deal with the bad guys—we officers understand that we are often dealing with normally law-abiding people. Sure, some are jerks, some are repeat offenders, but many are just motorists exercising their rights as Americans; we respect that.

But realize also, with regard to traffic infractions, that cops are generally accurate as to whether or not the infraction occurred—it's a significant part of what we do on a daily basis. While forms and procedures are constantly changing to keep up with the politics of the day, and officers can sometimes make simple data-entry or procedural errors—nonetheless, they still know what they saw.

Some judges will dismiss tickets for the slightest error or omission. Other judges understand that obvious innocuous omissions or petty errors do not change the nature or reality of the offense, and will convict despite the administrative error. This is luck of the draw and timing, and it's a fact that some drivers take their chances that luck will be on their side.

So, the cop's standing next to you—big deal:

This book is dedicated to those occasions when bad driving happens to good drivers, and specifically when Johnny Law's baby blues happen to be watching at the time. But there may be a time when you truly feel that the officer made a mistake and you find yourself in court fighting what you feel is an undeserved ticket. Don't let the officer's presence dissuade you. Keep in mind that he's been in traffic court before and he'll be there again; it's just another part of the job.

Oops! Did I really do that?

I can't emphasize enough the importance of being honest, first with yourself and then with the court. Before going to court, debrief yourself. Replaying the incident from your perspective is fine, but may not be as valuable as replaying it from the officer's perspective. Think about his location at the time he says you committed the infraction. This may give you a revelation that will prevent you from wasting your and the court's time, and save you that embarrassing epiphany in court when you suddenly realize, Uh-oh . . . I really did do that. *Doh!*

Fighting the good fight:

On the other hand, after debriefing yourself, you find the reasons why the officer's perspective may have been compromised and you take your findings to court and present them to the judge. You lay out your case in a sober and logical fashion, keeping emotion out of it, and basing your argument solely on facts. The judge may be impressed, or at least not annoyed, and just may see things your way. And don't be surprised if the officer shakes your hand and offers congratulations in the hallway afterward; after all, we can't win 'em all. Good luck!

YOUR ORAL WARNING:

"Don't lie. Don't be disrespectful. Use your right to remain silent if you don't want to incriminate yourself, but don't lie. And answer the questions the officer is asking you. If I ask, 'Where are you coming from?' don't tell me something other than where you're coming from!"

—Officer M. Wong, Seattle Police Department, Patrol

CHAPTER 25

A Final Oral Warning . . .

. . . And finally, there was peace on earth.

In this chapter . . .

☑ Common courtesy may get you further than you think

☑ Acting in ways against our intended goals

☑ Working on better communication all around

As we've worked our way to this point in the book, hopefully you've seen a trend emerge, a discernible pattern showing behavior that is likely to get you a ticket rather than get you off with a warning. Most lessons come down to common courtesy.

> ☑ **Blue Light Bulletin:** Common courtesy toward other motorists may keep you from getting stopped in the first place, and common courtesy toward the officer—if you do happen to get stopped—can keep you from getting a citation.

I remember when I was a kid coming of driving age in Massachusetts, the Commonwealth had a public-safety campaign that stated it so simply, but so elegantly: A LITTLE COURTESY WON'T KILL YOU. We'd all do well to adopt this axiom today.

This is not rocket science, brain surgery, or trying to program your Uncle Ned's combination VCR-coffeemaker; it's simple: *Act like your parents taught you to act when you were a little kid, or the way you teach your own children to behave with those in authority.*

You've noticed I've provided you with several stories, from simply peculiar to utterly bizarre, regarding how not to act if you want a warning (or, I suppose, how to act if a ticket is exactly what you're after). That's because how to act is easy and should be obvious to us, but too often it isn't. Sometimes we act in ways that are opposite to our intended goal, and we do it for all kinds of reasons.

Our egos are inflated:

Probably the biggest reason is ego. It's amazing how difficult it is for some people to admit when they're wrong. You may know some of them. You may be one of them. They have a hell of a time admitting when they're wrong or when they've made a mistake. It's often to their own detriment, because saying you're right, remaining adamant about your position, or refusing to give an inch, doesn't change the facts of a situation if you're wrong. To quote John Adams, "Facts are stubborn things; and whatever may be our wishes, our inclinations, or the dictates of our passion, they cannot alter the state of the facts and evidence." Gee, I couldn't have said it better myself (so I didn't). If you won't take it from me, take it from Mr. Adams.

> ☑ **Blue Light Bulletin:** The next time the cops stop you, lock your ego in the glove compartment. If it's that big, lock it in the trunk; and if you ride a motorcycle, lash it into the saddlebags. Do what you have to do to make wise decisions.

You're definitely asking for trouble if your ego is riding up front with you or clutching your waist from behind on your bike. It will nag at you and make you say and do things you'll regret, just like that boyfriend or girlfriend you dumped years ago. Remember, your ego doesn't have your best interests at heart; it acts on its own behalf—your well-being, be damned. The bottom line: Don't be a jerk. If you have to pretend you're not one, well, again, challenge yourself—make it a personal game. Besides, you can always inflate your ego again later.

A special request for this insider information:

This book's specific focus is on traffic interactions between motorists and cops; however, it also serves as an apt microcosm of the greater relationship between society and the police. The general public's lack of understanding of the police officer's complicated mission is astounding, but it's also quite under-standable. Unless you go through the police academy, go out into the field to conduct your patrol shift, and are on the blue side of the encounter, you can never fully appreciate the law enforce-ment officer's job. In lieu of this, we simply ask for the benefit of the doubt.

To most people what a police officer does seems simple, because they only see a small amount of it at a time. They see the police on a traffic stop or chasing a criminal or sitting in a coffee shop, chatting with other cops. They don't see the job's intrica-cies, the volume of knowledge a cop has to possess to do his job correctly. And this means not only knowing what he can, or must, do but also knowing what he *can't* do. He has to keep up with ever-changing court decisions, which can alter long-standing police procedures overnight.

There is also continuous training in criminal law, weapons proficiency, defensive tactics, emergency driving, hostage negoti-ations, crowd management (riot police training), CPR/First Aid/

AED training, and since 9/11, homeland security concerns. It's all in a day's work for a police officer.

> ☑ **Blue Light Bulletin:** Remember, we're talking about a job where, when the fists, blades, and bullets start to fly and everyone else has the good sense to run away from the violence, the cop runs toward it. He runs toward it, for low pay (when compared with other professions with lower risk), to help people he doesn't know, might not like, and who wouldn't cross the street to spit on him if he were on fire.

The odd thing to think about is, even petty tyrant Officer Ticketbook and rookie Officer Donnybrook would most likely risk their safety, even their lives, to save you. So again, even when you do encounter these law enforcement oddities, you might want to give them the benefit of the doubt. In fact, the way they see their jobs, in a strict, black-and-white way, should tell you that for them, the law is the law. Therefore, it also makes sense that their job is their job, and that job is to help you when you need it—regardless of how they feel about you.

Full-speed ahead . . . under 65 miles per hour, that is:

So, you want a warning, do you? Well, I don't blame you. You normally drive responsibly, you are considerate of other motorists, and you try to obey the traffic laws. But sometimes you've got a lot on your mind, you get distracted, or your normally good driving just lapses. You don't completely understand the nature of the officer's job, but you know it's difficult and you grant him the benefit of the doubt. That is commendable, and I agree; you should be rewarded. You may just have a good shot at that warning if you follow the advice I've provided in this book.

I haven't given you any information on how to lie to or dupe cops, or how to break the traffic laws without getting caught; people do enough of that without any help from me. This book is for the good motorists who find themselves caught at the wrong place at the wrong time, doing the wrong thing, and hope to get the benefit of the doubt from the officer, deputy, or trooper.

Aside from all that, don't you pay enough taxes already? Wouldn't you rather see your money go into something you want to buy instead of flowing into some municipal, county, or state coffer so they can buy a new radar gun, police motorcycle, or Cessna 182, just so they can catch you speeding again?

"Oh, Officer, don't you have anything better—" you begin.

Oh great, here it comes, the officer steels himself.

"—to do than to stop a nimrod like me? I'm sorry; I should have been paying more attention. I won't be doing that again. I'm sorry to waste your valuable time."

Well, do you think I'm gonna give you that warning you're hoping for? Sorry; please press hard—four copies! Just kidding. You betcha! Now, drive carefully and have a nice day.

YOUR (THIS-IS-IT) ORAL WARNING:

"The attitude of the driver is easily 90 percent of the determining factor between a ticket or no ticket."
—Craig Nelson, Deputy U.S. Marshal, former Army MP, Traffic Unit

Afterword

The primary lessons in this book are incredibly simple ones: Be honest, be respectful, and be nice. However, most of us don't receive such simple messages as an epiphany, or we immediately dismiss them as some naive platitudes. That's why I decided to use a combined delivery method to get this information out to you. I employ multiple stories within multiple chapters, illustrating many individual and unique circumstances I thought of, participated in, or picked from my fellow officers' brains.

In life sometimes we only get certain lessons at certain times. Unfortunately, some of us never get them. Perhaps life tried to teach you a lesson when you were twenty-two, but it didn't take; you weren't ready for it. When the same or similar lesson came back around when you were thirty-two, forty-two, or even sixty-two, your life's experiences may have prepared you to accept the message. Everything clicked, made sense—finally took. You think back to your twenty-two-year-old self and wonder how the heck you could have been such a dolt. I shouldn't call you a dolt if you now get some of the lessons taught in this book. I should actually congratulate you, because until now, this book hasn't been available, and from here on out you'll have no more excuses.